The Politics
of Crime and
Criminal Justice

Perspectives in Criminal Justice 8

ABOUT THE SERIES

The Perspectives in Criminal Justice Series is designed to meet the research information needs of faculty, students, and professionals who are studying and working in the field of criminal justice. The *Series* will cover a wide variety of research approaches and issues related to criminal justice. The books are collections of articles not previously published, and each book will focus on specific themes, research topics, or controversial issues.

The articles selected for publication are revised versions of papers presented at the annual meetings of the Academy of Criminal Justice Sciences. Papers organized around a specific topic are reviewed by the book's editor and a panel of referees for comment and suggestions for revision. The *Series* will rely on a multidisciplinary approach to such topical areas as organizational theory and change, the nature of crime, law and social control, and applied research as well as the traditional areas of police, courts, corrections, and juvenile justice.

The current volumes include:

— *Corrections at the Crossroads: Designing Policy,* edited by Sherwood E. Zimmermann and Harold D. Miller
— *Race, Crime, and Criminal Justice,* edited by R. L. McNeely and Carl E. Pope
— *Coping with Imprisonment,* edited by Nicolette Parisi
— *Managing Police Work: Issues and Analysis,* edited by Jack R. Greene
— *Police at Work: Policy Issues and Analysis,* edited by Richard R. Bennett
— *Corporations as Criminals,* edited by Ellen Hochstedler
— *Juvenile Justice Policy: Analyzing Trends and Outcomes,* edited by Scott H. Decker
— *The Politics of Crime and Criminal Justice,* edited by Erika S. Fairchild and Vincent J. Webb
— *Courts and Criminal Justice: Emerging Issues,* edited by Susette M. Talarico

Comments and suggestions from our readers are encouraged and welcomed.

Series Editor
John A. Conley
Criminal Justice Program
University of Wisconsin—Milwaukee

Perspectives in Criminal Justice 8

The Politics of Crime and Criminal Justice

Edited by
Erika S. Fairchild
Vincent J. Webb

*Published in cooperation with
the Academy of Criminal Justice Sciences*

SAGE PUBLICATIONS
Beverly Hills London New Delhi

1985

For information address:

SAGE Publications, Inc.
275 South Beverly Drive
Beverly Hills, California 90212

SAGE Publications India Pvt. Ltd.
M-32 Market
Greater Kailash I
New Delhi 110 048 India

SAGE Publications Ltd
28 Banner Street
London EC1Y 8QE
England

Printed in the United States of America

Library of Congress Cataloging in Publication Data
Main entry under title:

The politics of crime and criminal justice

(Perspectives in criminal justice; 8)
  1. Crime and criminals—United States.   2. Criminal justice, Administration of—United States.   3. Crime and criminals—Political aspects—United States.   4. Criminal justice, Administration of—Political aspects—United States.   I. Fairchild, Erika S.   II. Webb, Vincent J.
III. Series: Perspectives in criminal justice; 8.
HV6789.P58   1985   364'.973   84-27590
ISBN 0-8039-2423-2
ISBN 0-8039-2424-0 (pbk.)

FIRST PRINTING

CONTENTS

INTRODUCTION:
Crime, Justice, and Politics in the United States Today

Erika S. Fairchild
North Carolina State University
Vincent J. Webb
University of Nebraska at Omaha

This volume is about politics, crime, and criminal justice in the United States. As such, it reports on some of the fruits of an increasing amount of research that has been devoted to this topic in recent years. With the exception of one analytical essay on crime as an issue in American politics, all of the chapters in the volume are based on original field research.

"Politics" in this case refers to the relations of power and influence that occur between, on the one hand, those who are professionally involved—either in the private or the public sector—in the prevention of crime or in the processing of the accused and convicted and, on the other hand, those who are part of the complex representative decision-making apparatus that is called the political system in this country. This political system includes the public as electors, their representatives in legislative bodies at all levels of government, and their elected representatives in executive positions. This rather conventional approach to politics is adopted to avoid the conceptual and analytical confusion that results from the tendency to characterize all power and influence relations within organizations as the politics of the organization. Although this latter, more inclusive approach may also be termed "politics" and, as such, has been frequently adopted in writing about the criminal justice system, in this volume the focus is placed on some of the excellent research that is being done in the area of politics and criminal justice narrowly defined. The subject falls naturally into two categories: (1) politics and crime and (2) politics and criminal justice.

POLITICS AND CRIME

Crime involves breaking the social contract designed to make human relations reasonably predictable and nonthreatening. Crime as a social issue touches deep fears, insecurities, and emotions in most people. It also has religious and/or ethical dimensions that serve to heighten the intensity of feeling. At the most basic level, the control of predatory crime vies with defense against foreign predators as the first order of business of any government. It is always a part of the political agenda.

In the United States, however, crime as a policy issue has had periods of more or less concentration or visibility in the political arena. Those who say that the nation has been going through a period of the politicization of crime are suggesting that crime, for various reasons, is now more prominent on the political agenda than it normally is or even than the actual seriousness of the problem would require. The term "politicization" also suggests that crime and the fear of crime are being used by politicians as issues in which rhetorical and symbolic policy initiative can enhance their popularity and elect-ability. More radical scholars even claim that the crime issue is created by the ruling elite in order to mask the real problems of social decay, unemployment, and alienation that plague society (Quinney, 1973). Nevertheless, polls reveal that crime is one of the major concerns of the public. Interestingly, this is more so with forced choice questions (e.g., "How important are the following problems in the United States today?") than with open-ended ones (e.g., "What are the most important problems the United States faces today?"). With open-ended questions, other policy concerns (the economy, war, and peace) take precedence whereas with forced choice questions, crime has tended to have salience. Stuart Scheingold (1984: 44) in *The Politics of Law and Order* concludes that this difference "signals a powerful current of suggestibility within the public when it comes to crime"—a suggestibility that can be easily exploited by politicians.

⌈The seemingly intractable nature of the crime problem, coupled with increasing public concern because of the rising crime rates, has made crime a peculiarly frustrating policy problem for decision makers. Even more than in other policy areas, simple solutions are embraced with great enthusiasm, showered with attention and effort for a time, and then discarded amid bitter recriminations when the inevitable disappointment with the lack of clear-cut results sets in. The problem of overpromising and undersupporting also seems to be endemic to this policy area.⌋

⌈There is a peculiar dilemma here. At times when crime is not highly visible as a political issue, the whole apparatus of crime control and processing of the accused and convicted falls into disrepair and neglect. The fairness or justice, which the system most basically is supposed to be engendering, becomes increasingly problematical. At times when crime is highly visible on the political agenda, however, new problems take over. Increased resources for law enforcement bring the "dark figure" of unreported crime increasingly to light, thus making the increased enforcement efforts seem nonproductive. The basic inhumanity and unfairness of the processing system receive greater attention and resources, but the lack of understanding of the causes of and solutions for crime as a social issue makes these increased resources appear to be ineffective. The result is a trend toward punitiveness among policymakers, a punitiveness founded on feelings of frustration, anxiety, and loss of control. ⌋

POLITICS AND THE
CRIMINAL JUSTICE SYSTEM

One way to categorize the present situation in relation to politics and the criminal justice system would be to say that the country is going through a post-Progressive era in each of the components of the system: corrections, police, and courts. Post-Progressive means that a certain backlash against the reforms of the Progressive period in American life and politics, roughly the first fifty years of the twentieth century, is occurring and is resulting in renewed efforts to influence the system through political and public controls.

The Progressive era, as it affected the workings of the criminal justice system, was characterized by increasing reliance on bureaucratic solutions to policy problems. The effort was to downgrade politics, to emphasize the importance of training and expertise, and to make professionalism a rallying cry for increased responsibility for administrators. Concomitant with all this were also greater amounts of discretion delegated to the professionals in the system. The Progressive philosophy worked itself out in diverse ways in the various components of the criminal justice system but was neverthe-less evident in each one. Likewise, post-Progressivism has distinctive traits in each sector.

In the correctional system, the emphasis of Progressivism was on remedies tailored to the needs of individuals rather than on formal legal rules. The prototypical correctional structures were probation, parole, and juvenile courts. The essential faith of the Progressives was in the ability of the new disciplines of psychology and sociology to lead the way, not only to better understanding of offenders but also to better ways to deal with them. The vehicles for effecting these outcomes were bureaucratic structures in which well-trained indi-viduals would practice the kind of discretion that would lead to individual programs of rehabilitation for each offender (Rothman, 1980; Ryerson, 1979).

The reaction to the Progressive rehabilitative philosophy in correc-tions is well known by now. For the past fifteen years, academics, legislators, and correctional personnel have been going through a major reappraisal of the goals, practices, and accomplishments of corrections in this country. The changes have emphasized greater political involvement in the system, chiefly through the passage of determinate sentencing laws but also through legislative authoriza-tion of new prisons and through court initiatives on prison conditions.

In law enforcement, although Progressivism was also manifested by a crusade to divorce the system from political control, it was a different kind of political control, that of big city machine politics that awarded police positions as a form of patronage and that winked at police corruption in exchange for police cooperation with machine goals. Progressive police reformers called for the kind of profes-sionalism in which power was lodged predominantly in the chiefs of departments and in which training, discipline, and impartiality in enforcing the law were stressed. This was not less a bureaucratic solution to policy problems but one in which discretion was designed to be lodged more obviously in the higher levels of the bureaucracy (Fogelson, 1977; Walker, 1979).

Post-Progressivism in policing has been characterized by emphasis on closer ties between police and public and less social and occupational isolation, and greater accountability of the police. A new professionalism, one that stresses responsible street-level discretionary behavior in tune to community service needs, is being fostered (Goldstein, 1977).

Even in the field of court administration, the Progressive reforms called for bureaucratic as opposed to legalistic approaches to problems of delay, inefficiency, and political interference. The founding of the American Judicature Society, the development of an administrative office of the courts at the federal level and then gradually in the states, and the push toward unitary court systems within states are all examples of these approaches. Again the problems were different from those faced by police and by corrections authorities, but the proposed solutions had in common the faith in merit, efficiency, and nonpolitical solutions to operating problems within the court system.

Centralization and bureaucratization were not found to be cure-alls for the problems of the courts, however, which continued to be plagued by overcrowding, a sense of marginal dispensation of justice, and alienation of offenders, victims, witnesses, and attorneys. As in the other two components of the criminal justice system, the recent trend in the courts has been toward greater accountability to the public. This has been manifested by decentralization of administrative functions through the use of trial court administrators in some jurisdictions, through attempts to regularize the plea bargaining process, and through programs, such as victim-witness coordinator programs, and neighborhood justice centers aimed at decreasing alienation of the public and the participants in the system.

In this dialectic of pre-Progressivism, Progressivism, and post-Progressivism, the talk of post-Progressivism seems premature to many professionals in the system who claim that the Progressive reforms themselves have not been implemented with any regularity or enthusiasm. Nevertheless, the post-Progressive era is characterized by the attempt to reestablish political accountability. As one of the chapters in this volume explains, however, a definite line is to be drawn between political accountability and political interference (Guyot). Post-Progressivism is not meant to imply a return to corruption, political patronage, and usurpation of control of the system by politicians. Rather, it is meant to counter some of the effects of what are perceived as the irresponsible aspects of bureaucratic discretion.

THE LITERATURE OF POLITICS,
CRIME, AND CRIMINAL JUSTICE

If post-Progressivism does in fact proclaim a greater political responsibility of the criminal justice system, then a study is appropriate of the complex relationships between the actors in the various subsystems and political decision makers, including the public. To be sure, crime, as a major policy problem of federal, state, and local governments, has always had political ramifications. Until recent years, however, the politics of crime and criminal justice has been neglected as a field of scholarly endeavor. At least one reason for this neglect is probably that, before the advent of large numbers of multidisciplinary programs in criminal justice in the 1970s, criminal justice was not frequently taught or emphasized among political scientists, who would be those most likely to engage in such studies. Another reason may well be that until recently, research money has gone largely into applied areas involving development of baseline data and evaluation of experimental programs. The more basic, complex, and less controllable aspects of criminal justice policy gave way to projects that, at least in theory, were more amenable to results of some kind. As the optimism of the early 1970s has given way to the frustrating realization that crime is a more intractable problem than had been thought by those who made criminal justice policy, the issue of the policy-making process itself has come increasingly to the fore.

This is not to say that research into the relations between politics and criminal justice had not been done before 1975. *Varieties of Police Behavior,* James Q. Wilson's (1968) study of the relation between political culture and style of policing, is an important example of such earlier work. In the area of policing also, Leonard Ruchelman's (1974) study of the relations between police and mayors in three cities was a noteworthy contribution as was Alan Bent's (1974) study of politics and policing. In the area of courts, Levin's (1977) study of political culture and judicial style is particularly interesting. Other works, especially those by historians, could be mentioned. (For a more complete summary and bibliography of political and criminal justice see Nagel et al., 1983, especially the introductions to the various sections.)

In recent years, however, some large-scale, well-funded studies of the political correlates of criminal justice policy have appeared. At the state level, the studies of Berk and Rossi (1977) and of Berk, Brachman, and Lesser (1977) are noteworthy. Berk and Rossi used a survey method to probe state leadership opinion on prison reform in Washington, Illinois, and Florida. The fact that their research was done in the early 1970s may appear to date their finding that the rehabilitative ideal has reasonably strong support among state legislators. In fact, the research described by Cullen et al. in the present volume suggests at least that legislators are not as single-minded in their values as might be supposed from the punitive nature of much recent criminal justice legislation. Berk, Brachman, and Lesser studied all changes in the criminal law in the state of California from 1960-1972. This complex study used content analysis, historical research, and interviews in order to develop a better understanding of the forces that influence the passage of particular laws. Their description of the cooperation among ostensibly competing groups and the minimal involvement of the public or of public opinion in the legislative process concerned with criminal law is based on the peculiarities of the situation in California. Nevertheless, it provides a benchmark for other studies of the lawmaking process in relation to criminal justice.

At the urban level, the Governmental Responses to Crime project at Northwestern University intensively studied no less than ten major cities in order to develop a better understanding of the relations among local political cultures, local history, and criminal justice outcomes. This project concluded that the failure of crime policy is related to such factors as extreme fragmentation of the system, attempts to find local solutions to an essentially national problem, and lack of knowledge about successful crime fighting techniques. In the meantime, responses to the crime problem appear to have been a factor in local politics in the cities studied (Jacob, 1984).

Broad generalizations are impossible to make from the studies that have been done. No one ruling viewpoint appears to have developed unless it is that the policymaking process in criminal justice is closely related to particulars of local political culture. In fact, one of the authors in this volume (Duffee) suggests just that: On the one hand, exemplary projects may not be replicable from one community to another, but, on the other hand, almost any project can work, given the political-social conditions hospitable to its development.

In any case, more precise generalizations must await the results of further studies. Regional studies of particular policy areas like sentencing, for example, might prove fruitful in the search for a more encompassing theory. One problem with the present literature in this field is that it tends to be specific to only one state or locality or else that the randomly chosen multiple jurisdictions have left out the possibility of finding strong regional regularities.

THE CONTRIBUTIONS OF
THIS VOLUME

The research described in this volume encompasses a sizable number of jurisdictions and approaches to the study of politics, crime, and criminal justice through both single case studies and aggregate research. Because of the subject matter, almost half of the volume is concerned with legislative politics at the state and federal levels. In the area of institutional politics are three case studies, two on local politics and police and one on state politics and corrections.

The first chapter is an analysis of crime as an issue in American politics by Joel Rosch. Rosch argues that the ideological parameters of the law and order debate were established in the latter 1960s and have determined the nature of the politics of crime and justice ever since. He concludes that this historical reality has not served well the needs of either the general public or the victims of crime.

The second section of the volume is concerned with legislative politics. Albert Melone builds on his previous research on the American Bar Association and on federal criminal code reform to describe the nature of the intervention and influence practiced by the ABA in the passage of federal criminal law. Because of the wealth and prestige of its members, the ABA is a particularly powerful interest group in the criminal justice field. One of the peculiarities of this policy field, however, is that the major interest groups in general are those of the professionals in the system: lawyers, police, judges, sheriffs, correctional personnel, and so on. Clients of the system, such as offenders, victims, witnesses, and even the general public, are represented, if at all, by surrogate organizations such as the ACLU and various church groups. This makes for a certain imbalance in the competition for legislator attention. Melone's chapter provides valuable insight into the intricacies of interest articulation in relation to criminal law.

Both Melone's chapter and the one by Cullen, Bynum, Greene, and Garrett challenge some stereotypes about the politics of criminal justice. Cullen et al. have found a greater diversity of opinion among legislators than might be surmised from an examination of their voting records on criminal law. Melone writes that the record of Congressional accordance with ABA preference on criminal code reform suggests a more mixed kind or degree of influence than presumed by those who think that the ABA has overwhelming influence in Congress.

These two studies show that the ambiguities and complexities of power and influence in relation to criminal justice policy are in need of considerable research before a clearer understanding of predictable patterns of behavior is gained.

The chapter by Anne Heinz relies on some of the data gathered for the Governmental Responses to Crime project for which she served as project director. Heinz is also building on the work in newspaper content analysis in the California study by Berk, Brachman, and Lesser. Her analysis of the nature of interest group involvement in criminal justice and the importance of newspaper opinion both as a lobbying and an agenda-setting force is an important contribution to the development of knowledge in interest articulation in criminal justice. This study is thoroughly professional in its approach to social science as an incremental science in which the findings of previous researchers are refined, explored further, or disproved.

The final section of the volume turns to another form of criminal justice politics: the relation between "outside" political forces and the bureaucratic entities that make up the system. Two studies are included on the politics of police department operations plus a thought-provoking examination of the effect of politics on prerelease programs. David Duffee's case study of a Pennsylvania prerelease program and his comparison of it with those in several other states is rich in the development of the interplay between theory and practice. A disturbing aspect of his conclusion is that success or failure, or even the developing nature of a particular program, has a certain random quality. Nevertheless, Duffee himself sees at least typological regularities in the process and presents them in terms of types of programs and community political fields.

If post-Progressivism involves a movement toward greater political accountability on the part of criminal justice agencies, the line between accountability and interference becomes especially important if the excesses and corruptions of the pre-Progressive period are to be avoided. Dorothy Guyot makes an original and interesting contribution to the understanding of this border area in her case study of political attempts to influence the chief of one police department in the state of New York. Her case study is distinctive for its development of the theory of accountability in relation to the ideas about evaluation of police performance developed by Whitaker et al. in a 1980 report. It is also distinctive because of her analysis of the relationships between the various facets of the evaluation model and the actual situation in Troy.

Finally, Samuel Walker's case study of the Seattle police spying ordinance also tells something important about political account- ability and criminal justice operations. Walker makes clear that accountability cannot easily be based on coercion but depends upon a cooperative relationship between the parties involved. Walker also contributes to knowledge about a matter that is making headlines in other cities: official record keeping on noncriminal organizational or protest activities by citizens. The Seattle ordinance is an unusual attempt to assert public control over police activities through the use of an auditor of police case records. Walker shows the interplay of the elements of political ripeness, interest group involvement, general political culture, and institutional responsiveness in the successful development and implementation of political rule making for the regulation of a government agency.

REFERENCES

BENT, A. (1974) The Politics of Law Enforcement. Lexington, MA: D.C. Heath.

BERK, R. and P. ROSSI (1977) Prison Reform and State Elites. Cambridge, MA: Ballinger.

BERK, R., H. BRACHMAN, and S. LESSER (1977) As Measure of Justice. New York: Academic Press.

FOGELSON, R. (1977) Big City Police. Cambridge, MA: Harvard University Press.

GOLDSTEIN, H. (1977) Policing a Free Society. Cambridge, MA: Ballinger.

JACOB, H. (1984) The Frustration of Policy: Responses to Crime by American Cities. Boston: Little, Brown.

LEVIN, M. (1977) Urban Politics and the Criminal Courts. Chicago: University of Chicago Press.

NAGEL, S., E. FAIRCHILD, and A. CHAMPAGNE [eds.] (1983) The Political Science of Criminal Justice. Springfield, IL: Charles C Thomas.

QUINNEY, R. (1973) Critique of Legal Order. Boston: Little, Brown.

ROTHMAN, D. (1980) Conscience and Convenience. Boston: Little, Brown.

RUCHELMAN, L. (1974) Police Politics. Cambridge, MA: Ballinger.

RYERSON, E. (1979) The Best-Laid Plans. New York: Hill and Wang.

SCHEINGOLD, S. (1984) The Politics of Law and Order. New York: Longman.

WALKER, S. (1979) A Critical History of Police Reform. Lexington, MA: D.C. Heath.

WILSON, J. Q. (1968) Varieties of Police Behavior. Cambridge, MA: Harvard University Press.

I.

Crime and Politics

1.

CRIME AS AN ISSUE IN AMERICAN POLITICS

Joel Rosch

North Carolina State University

For two decades our nation has fought a "war on crime" and lost. Between 1968 and 1981 the federal government spent more than 8 billion dollars on crime through the Law Enforcement Assistance Act (LEAA), while state and local government spent 25 to 30 times more (Cronin et al., 1981). Despite these efforts, fluctuations in crime rates still seem beyond the control of public policy. Gerald Chaplan, law school professor and former research director for LEAA summed up this failure in an article entitled "Losing the War on Crime" (in Cronin et al., 1981: 181).

> First, we have more crime than any other place in the world, more this year than last, and much, much more than we had in 1964 when Senator Goldwater became the first Presidential candidate to argue that the Federal government must do something about crime in the streets.

> Second, most of the increase occurred in the midst of high employment and unprecedented affluence and during a period when the Federal government launched a new, multi-billion dollar anti-crime program.

> Third, despite the persistent, often clarion, calls for "law and order," no significant strengthening of the punitive or deterrence features of the criminal justice system took place during the past decade.

> Fourth, efforts to understand better the underlying causes of crime have progressed little. Even among serious observers, the attachment to particular explanations has been promiscuous, one theory yielding to another in quick succession.

> Fifth, today virtually no one—scholars, practitioners and politicians alike—dares to advance a program which promises to reduce crime substantially in the near future.

A number of explanations have been offered for the failure of criminal justice policy. The explanations include the nature of crime itself (Erickson, 1966), a lack of resources and commitment (Reiman, 1979), weaknesses in American culture (Wilson, 1975; Cronin et al., 1981), and the nature of American federalism (Cronin et al., 1981). Some blame stingy conservative legislatures for failing to attack the "root causes" of crime (Zeisel, 1982). Others blame liberal judges and liberal policies for handcuffing the police and weakening the moral bonds that used to restrain criminal behavior (Harris, 1970; Carrington, 1975).

The argument in this chapter is that the war on crime failed in part because of the way crime emerged on the American political agenda in the late 1960s and 1970s. What will be described as the "political scenario" associated with crime prevented the formation of coalitions to press for policies that might have addressed the problems faced by citizens most often victimized by crime.

LIBERAL AND CONSERVATIVE APPROACHES TO THE PROBLEM OF CRIME

Although the issue of crime has long played a part in local politics in the United States, it first began to occupy a significant place in national politics during the mid-1960s (Jacob and Lineberry, 1982a: 6). The 1964 presidential election was the first in which crime was a major issue on the national political agenda (Cronin et al., 1981; Baker, 1983). By 1968, law and order rhetoric had become a staple of conservative political campaigns. In that year, it was used extensively by Richard Nixon in his successful presidential campaign (Baker, 1983: 38-40). Because street crime increased rapidly during this period, the fact that crime became an important political issue is not surprising (Jacob and Lineberry, 1982a). What is curious is the way crime was used in political debate.

Crime is something all groups in the political process are against. Conflict arises over what to do about crime and, more important for this chapter, what the nature of the crime problem really is (Jacob and Lineberry, 1982a). Before 1960, crime itself was not a major concern of most citizens. For liberals who usually claim to speak for lower-class groups, the problems of the criminal justice system traditionally have centered on concerns about due process of law and the rights of defendants rather than on crime control (Wilson, 1975; Stolz, 1983). Abuses in the criminal justice system are spoken of as the abuses of defendants' rights (Ryan, 1976). Discrimination is usually spoken of as the overzealous enforcement of the law against lower-class groups. Prior to the 1960s when the amount of crime in society became a major political issue, the problem of how defendants were treated seemed more pressing than the problem of crime.

Since the Progressive era, liberal reformers have attempted to improve the criminal justice system by making sure the procedures used by the police, the courts, and corrections conformed to notions of fairness and due process of law. Progressive reformers found gross inequalities in the workings of trial courts and local police agencies. Early empirical studies found evidence of systematic discrimination against lower-class individuals and members of minority groups as well as evidence of widespread police brutality (Hofstadter, 1955; Rumble, 1968; Lowi, 1979; Green, 1961).

In a series of court cases beginning in the 1930s, liberal reformers called on the federal courts to ensure that local police and local courts gave equal protection to the rights of all defendants. After a long struggle, the 1960s saw the Warren Court expanding federal standards of due process of law and applying these standards to local law enforcement agencies through the Fourteenth Amendment (Baker, 1983).

Liberals have treated the rights of defendants as if they were pure public goods. Giving people their rights has not been seen as involving zero-sum or intergroup conflict. Rights have not been treated as if they were scarce in the sense that they have to be taken away from someone in order to give them to someone else. Expanding the rights of defendants has been seen as benefiting the whole society without imposing costs on any particular group (Lowi, 1964, 1970, 1972).

Liberals have seen crime itself as a function of failed social arrangements (Clark, 1970; Schur, 1969). Generations of progressive criminologists have shown that crime was caused by poverty, unemployment, discrimination, and other aspects of American society. Crime was to be lowered by changes in social and economic policies. The idea that crime was caused by biological or racial factors was seen as an especially dangerous one. If criminal activity was shown to be a natural characteristic of a particular group, that group might be singled out for discriminatory treatment (Lindersmith and Levin, 1937).

While there may not be enough public defenders, judges, or adequate jail space, liberals seek to ensure that specific groups, such as blacks or poor people, are not being systematically denied their rights. The challenge faced by the criminal justice system is to see that all of those accused of committing crimes are treated equally and according to due process of law.

Opponents of the extension of due process traditionally made two kinds of arguments. The first was based on federalism. Criminal justice has traditionally been the province of local government. Although the federal courts ought to protect citizens from gross and obvious violations of due process, the federal courts have no right to impose national standards on local law enforcement agencies (Harlan, 1968).

The second argument was that the expansion of due process by the federal courts was imposing impossible burdens on local law enforcement agencies. Catching, trying, and convicting criminals was becoming too difficult. As long as crime remained relatively low, or at least was not perceived as a major social problem, the second argument did not attract as much attention as the first.

When crime started to become an important political issue in the 1960s, conservatives claimed that liberal policies were preventing law enforcement agencies from protecting society from crime. Less attention was paid to questions of federalism and more was paid to questions about reducing crime. Conservatives eventually called for an increased federal role in fighting crime.

For conservatives, debate about crime usually involves questions about scarce resources. Conservatives had traditionally been more sympathetic to the idea that crime is an inevitable part of society and that some groups are more prone to crime than others (Lindersmith and Levin, 1937). If crime were natural to society, reducing crime could only occur by making catching and punishing criminals easier for law enforcement agencies. Liberal policies, in particular those of the Warren Court, were said to protect the rights of defendants at the expense of everyone else.

While conservative "law and order" campaigns proved to be vague about how to make people safer, they were filled with "us" versus "them" rhetoric. A constant theme was one of giving government back to those who worked hard and paid their taxes (Scammon and Wattenberg, 1970). Stricter law enforcement would put the bad people behind bars and make the good people safe again. For conservatives, debate about crime involved questions of scarcity and group conflict. The issue of crime became one of whose interests were being served—those inclined to break the law or those who obey it.

Liberals talked about equality but only as it applied to defendants. Their fear was that a particular group of defendants would be treated unequally because of either prejudice or incorrect notions about the causes of crime. Equity questions were not applied to the victims of crime, except insofar as some criminals were spoken of as the "real victims" (Ryan, 1976).

For conservatives, the issue of crime did not involve questions about equity. Instead, the focus was on making the society as a whole safer. Those who spoke about equity for defendants were seen as protecting those who broke the law. The problem faced by the criminal justice system was to reestablish a proper balance between a few bad people and the rest of society. Conservatives spoke about victims, but the victim was society as a whole. No equity questions were raised about how any particular groups were treated, either as victims or as defendants.

THE PROBLEM OF
RISING CRIME RATES

The problems of the criminal justice system in the 1960s and 1970s, however, transcended the admittedly major difficulties faced by lower-class defendants. There was also too much crime, and the burden of that crime fell disproportionately on the poor and on members of minority groups (Gurr, 1982). Although poor defendants may have been denied their rights, the vast majority of law abiding poor people were not given adequate protection from crime (Wilson, 1975).

The degree to which the poor and members of minority groups suffer unequally from crime is staggering. Herbert Packer estimated that the urban poor were 100 times more likely to be the victims of violent crimes than suburbanites. Blacks as a group constitute about 12 percent of the population but make up 55 percent of the murder victims (Carrington, 1975). In 1970, murder was the fourth leading cause of death among black males.

Victimization surveys show that for all serious crimes, blacks report a higher rate of victimization than whites, people with incomes below $3,000 a greater rate than those with incomes above $3,000, and the unemployed 2 or 3 times the rate of those employed (Platt, 1981). Blacks suffer aggravated assault at twice the rates whites do and are twice as likely to be robbed. Among those robbed, twice as many blacks are injured and 3 times as many suffer serious injuries, according to the U.S. Department of Justice (1976). While violent crime in the United States went up 336 percent from 1965 to 1974 (Skogan and Maxfield, 1981), the rate at which white Americans were victimized remained relatively constant (Gurr, 1982). There is good evidence to believe that almost all the increase in murder and aggravated assault was experienced by black Americans (Gurr, 1982).

Poor people and members of minority groups clearly understood the degree to which they suffered unequally from crime (Scammon and Wattenberg, 1970). In a 1974 survey, 66 percent of all blacks and 64 percent of those earning under $10,000 listed crime as the problem they would most want to see government address (Burnham, 1974). Even more than whites, blacks felt that more should be done to punish those who broke the law (Fowler, 1974). Regardless of race or class, crime is the issue in which there is the greatest agreement that more government action is appropriate and necessary (Burnham et al., 1974; Saunders, 1976; Brown, 1972). While liberals worried about the rights of defendants and conservatives spoke about the overall level of crime and disorder in society, the greatest cause of dissatisfaction with the criminal justice system among poor people and members of minority groups was the belief that their lives and property did not receive the same protection given to upper-class groups (Campbell et al., 1976; Anton and Bowen, 1976; Jacob, 1971, 1972).

Although a reduction in crime would have been in the interests of the lower classes, perhaps equally important would have been a change in what Lance Bennett (1975: 23-25; n.d.: 35-41) has called the "political scenario" associated with crime:

> Political scenarios dictate how bits of information fit together, which bits are more significant than others, and which bits should be included in or excluded from a satisfactory conceptualization of the issue.

> We should not take the perceptual power of contextualization lightly. . . . The ability to locate "scenic containers" which establish preferred configurations of these terms is the cornerstone of political success.

Although groups are generally expected to act in their own interests, how people come to understand their interests can be influenced by the way events take on meaning in the course of political debate

(Carson, 1974). To understand the anti-crime policies that came out of the "war on crime," an understanding is necessary of how the political scenario associated with crime was constructed.

SETTING THE
POLITICAL AGENDA: THE RISE OF
LAW AND ORDER POLITICS

Barry Goldwater first used the issue of crime in the 1964 political campaign at the urging of Richard Kleindienst (Baker, 1983). Kleindienst and other Goldwater strategists understood that crime could symbolize more than people being robbed or assaulted. They believed that the crime issue would enable them to speak to the general feeling many Americans had about the growing disorder and perceived anarchy in American society (Baker, 1983). When Goldwater spoke about "crime," he spoke about general social unrest, a permissive court, and a deteriorating society. He did not speak about programs to reduce the number of murders or robberies. He did not speak about who was victimized by crime. Goldwater's campaign strategists hoped to portray their candidate as someone who, by being tough on crime, would put an end to the growing chaos in American society (Cronin et al., 1981). This pitch was directed mostly at "middle American" and especially suburban voters (Cronin et al., 1981; Baker, 1983).

The Kerner Commission later showed that crime, civil rights, urban riots, and political protests were all bound together in the public mind. Commenting about 1964, Baker (1983: 42) notes, "race and crime were often scrambled in the public mind, their common denominator, fear—fear of being mugged on a street corner and fear of being mugged economically by the newcomer in the labor market." Whether Goldwater intended to use the public's growing concern about crime and disorder against those interested in civil rights, civil rights leaders came to understand the call for "law and order" as a call for an end to progress in civil rights (Cronin et al., 1981). The head of the NAACP feared the "law and order" campaigns enough to call for a moratorium on demonstrations during the 1964 elections (Cronin et al., 1981). Although Goldwater lost the 1964 presidential election, he succeeded in setting the scene for debate about crime. During this period, the issue of crime became closely associated with civil rights, urban riots, lifestyle changes, and a general feeling about disorder (Jacob and Lineberry, 1982a).

The Democratic candidate, and landslide winner in the 1964 presidential elections, Lyndon Johnson understood Goldwater's use of the crime issue as a traditional conservative objection to the courts' imposition of national standards of due process on local law enforcement agencies as well as an attack on progress made in the field of civil rights (Cronin et al., 1981). Consistent with traditional liberal beliefs, Johnson was uncomfortable with arguments about law enforcement policies designed to reduce crime. He preferred to talk about social programs that would attack the "root causes" of crime. Johnson believed that his "war on poverty" was the most effective way to fight crime (Cronin et al., 1981). When he did talk about crime, he advocated programs such as increased funds for the police and more training for other criminal justice workers. Johnson did not, however, pay as much attention to crime as Goldwater did (Baker, 1983).

After the 1964 election, anti-war protests, controversial Supreme Court decisions, and the increase in urban disorder kept the issue of crime (as Goldwater had defined it) a central issue in American politics. Between 1965 and 1967, over 100 cities experienced urban disorders. In 1966 the Miranda decision was portrayed in most popular accounts as tying the hands of law enforcement by allowing the guilty to go free on technicalities. George Wallace pointed out that the same Supreme Court that had ordered integration and encouraged civil rights protests was now bending over backward to help criminals. Wallace constantly raised the law and order issue in the period before the 1968 presidential elections, always linking crime with anti-war protests, civil rights, the Supreme Court, and liberal social programs (Baker, 1983; Cronin et al., 1981).

Crime also rose dramatically, and by 1968 offenses against persons showed a 106 percent increase from 1960 (Scammon and Wattenberg, 1970). More important, by 1968 over 75 percent of the U.S. public believed that law and order had broken down and that a new president could do something about the problem (Scammon and Wattenberg, 1970). The effects of crime were felt most directly by the lower classes and especially by those living in older declining cities, the traditional constituency of the Democratic party (Jacob and Lineberry, 1982b). The Democrats continued to respond to the crime issue as they had in the past, advocating programs aimed at issues such as housing, education, and discrimination. Although those programs may have addressed the "root causes" of crime, they seemed to favor those groups Goldwater, and later Nixon and Wallace, blamed for the breakdown of order.

Although the rise in the crime rate became most visible at the same time that civil rights protests were attracting more attention, little evidence has been found that civil rights activity led to increased crime. All the evidence points in the other direction. Cities that had civil rights activity usually experienced a drop in crime during and after the protest (Soloman et al., 1980). However, the same news reports that carried stories about civil rights activity also documented the rise in crime (Jacob and Lineberry, 1982a; Cronin et al., 1981).

Crime was seen as the number one problem facing America by 48 percent of the population in 1965 and 63 percent in 1968 (Cronin et al., 1981). Public opinion polls showed that political assassinations, urban riots, civil rights protests, and anti-war protests were closely associated with the idea that crime was rising (even when it was not). Even if these events occurred thousands of miles away, they led people in communities that had little crime to become concerned about it (Rhodes, 1977). During the 1968 presidential campaign, both George Wallace and Richard Nixon made "law and order" a central theme in their campaigns. Although Nixon tried to distance himself from Wallace's harsh rhetoric linking crime and race, he understood that the issues were fused in the public mind (Cronin et al., 1981). Nixon promised to do something about "crime in the streets." Like Goldwater, his campaign was pitched to suburban voters and middle-class Americans, the people least likely to be victimized (Cronin et al., 1981). In political debate, opposing crime meant you were against the kind of people who created disorder.

The Democrats were never able to use the crime issue as well as the Republicans. The various commissions appointed by Lyndon Johnson to look at crime focused most of their attention on "root causes," and, except for advocating better training for law enforcement officials, offered no clear solutions to the problem of crime (Cronin et al., 1981). They reflected what Nixon and Wallace were to characterize as an undue concern for the criminal (Stolz, 1983). Wallace and Nixon focused on specific villains such as the Warren Court, a weak attorney general, and civil rights and anti-war protesters (Cronin et al., 1981).

By the end of the 1960s, 81 percent of the public believed that law and order had broken down and that Communists and blacks who started riots were the causes of the breakdown (Cronin et al., 1981). Civil rights marches and urban disorder increased the public's concern with crime (Jacob and Lineberry, 1982a). When crime was debated, it was more likely to be associated with "social issues" like school desegregation, race and ethnic relations, and civil disorders than with questions about the distribution of other urban services like housing, transportation, education, urban redevelopment, or even more germane topics such as how to deploy the police (Jacob and Lineberry, 1982a).

In *The Real Majority,* Scammon and Wattenberg (1970) show how effectively conservative politicians used the crime issue in national and local elections in 1968 and 1969. Those who argued for law and order rarely made specific proposals about how to reduce crime. When they talked about crime, they talked about the Warren Court, political demonstrations, the youth culture, and a host of other social issues. Those who used the law and order issue attracted votes from suburban and middle neighborhoods that had relatively little crime. They were able to win elections on the crime issue without having to talk about what they would do to increase the safety of those most often victimized by crime (Scammon and Wattenberg, 1970).

Former Attorney General Katzenbach has argued that even if we had had no civil rights revolutions, no Vietnam War, no furor about free speech, and no Warren Court, we still would have had a crime problem in the 1960s (Cronin et al., 1981). Most studies of the growth of crime bear out Katzenbach's observations (Wilson, 1975). These events, however, did occur. They occurred even as the problem of crime emerged on the national political agenda. Consequently, they became fused with crime in the public mind. They did not cause the rising crime rate, but they did create a political scenario that determined the way the problem of crime would be debated.

SYMBOLIC AND INSTRUMENTAL
ASPECTS OF CRIME POLICY

Those who used the crime issue most successfully in the 1960s and 1970s created a political scenario in which showing concern about crime was equated with concern about the disorder that characterized that period. Crime rose, but disorder was associated with civil rights, demonstrations, urban riots, and anti-war protests. Although little of this disorder had to do with the rise of murder, assault, rape, and burglary, it contributed to people's fear that crime was rising (Rhodes, 1977; Jacob and Lineberry, 1982a).

How are we to understand the way crime was used in political campaigns? Better and fairer law enforcement could have been debated as a need shared by all groups in society, especially the poor and members of minority groups. Instead, crime became an issue where, as Wilson (1975: 81) has observed:

> It became impossible to construct a political strategy that rested on finding what problems blacks and whites had in common. Politics, under the "white racism" doctrine, became a zero-sum game—anything blacks win, whites must lose, and vice versa.

Crime was conceptualized as an issue that involved conflict between those who created disorder and those who did not. Being against crime in the street came to mean that a politician was appealing to middle-class white voters. An anti-crime stance was perceived as an anti-black bias. Lower-class groups voted against "law and order" candidates despite the fact that they could have benefited the most from real reductions in crime (Scammon and Wattenberg, 1970).

The crime issue had become a symbol that evoked a series of images. The dominant ones included the urban rioter, the civil rights activist, the anti-war protester, the welfare cheat, as well as the mugger. The courts seemed to handcuff the police, and liberal do-gooders seemed to coddle criminals. Society appeared to do more and more for the criminal types and less and less for hard-working people who obeyed the laws. The liberal image of the poor defendant being denied his rights gave rise to less anger and political movement than the conservative picture of a society favoring those who created disorder over those who obeyed the law. For those who had the most to gain from real reductions in crime, neither scenario addressed the issue of making them safer.

The way in which the "political scenario" of crime developed resulted in a discontinuity between what John Gusfield (1963) has called symbolic and instrumental interests of those most often victimized by crime. Symbolic politics is concerned with status and public affirmations that a particular group is right or morally correct (Gusfield, 1963: 23). He states, "The fact of political victory against the enemy shows where social and political dominances lie. The legislative victory, whatever its factual consequences, confers respect and approval on its supporters." For Goldwater initially, and later Wallace and Nixon, opposing crime meant giving the country back to the "silent majority" who did not riot, protest, or break the law. The appeal to "law and order" and crime control, being so closely linked to issues of lifestyle, was a way of telling one group of Americans that they were right and that the others were wrong.

Instrumental politics refers to the allocation of material resources or the distribution of burdens and benefits in society. The heavy burden of the rise in crime during this period fell as it always had on the poor and members of minority groups. The interests of lower-class groups would have been served better by policies that reduced crime.

Expanding on Gusfield's analysis, John Carson (1974) has argued that most public policy questions contain both symbolic and material aspects. A divergence can exist between a group's symbolic and material interests. Groups with similar instrumental goals may find themselves at odds because of the way issues take on meanings in public debate (Carson, 1974). Understanding the interactions between symbolic and instrumental aspects of political campaigns can provide insight into the outcome of struggles over legislation.

Law and order politics became symbolic of status politics in the 1960s and 1970s. The issue of crime became a debate over whom the law served rather than how to reduce crime. The direct material benefits that the largely white middle-income voters derived from the specific policies toward crime advocated by Goldwater, Nixon, and Wallace were marginal at best (Harris, 1970). Arresting demonstrators, narrowing the scope of the Miranda decision, and increasing the use of wiretaps have had little impact on either crime or the fear of crime (Harris, 1970; Forst, 1983).

Crime rose but those who argued for law and order promised little in the way of protection from crime. Instead they offered policies that would, in Gusfield's (1963: 22) words, "show where social and political dominance lie." The victory of law and order candidates was "symbolic of the status and power of the cultures opposing each other. Legal affirmation or rejection is thus important in what it symbolizes as well or instead of what it controls. Even if the law was broken, it was clear whose law it was" (Gusfield, 1963: 67).

For over a decade, however, the people who responded to law and order campaigns had seen young people and black people flaunt the law and traditional values. Government seemed to listen to those who protested and broke the law. The courts had taken prayer out of the schools, ordered children to be bused, and was preoccupied with the rights of those who broke the law. It was time for the law to respond to the "good people."

The instrumental goals of those whose candidates lost to "law and order" candidates, however, would have been served by policies that really established law and order. The needs of those who would have benefited the most from programs to reduce crime were not served by the way the crime issue was used in political campaigns. To raise the crime issue came to mean that a person was anti-black or anti-poor.

Pol
victi
1983
deba
out o

Few pe
governme
1960s and
of this mo
training fo
Where libe
representat
humane. Th
crime were
increases in

liberal social programs. Evidence is scarce that cri
by taking the "handcuffs" off the police and bui
prisons (Wilson, 1983; Scheingold, 1983; 1
of the U.S. population appears to have h
crime rate than two decades of gov
1983).

The most promising program
getting citizens involved in t
police, prosecutors, and
1983; Hirsch, 1983; S
and George Kelli
direct contact
crime areas
on Amer
see c
(S

...... to
.......er the conservative
interest in or   ... ... concern with the rights of defendants
had much of an impact on the problem of crime, especially as it was
experienced by the poor.

Debate about crime in the 1980s shows more concern about
victims. In part this is due to the women's movement and heightened
concern about victims of rape (Platt, 1981; Cronin et al., 1981).
Recent research on victimization has increased awareness of the
degree to which lower-class people suffer disproportionately from
crime (Skogan and Maxfield, 1981). Black elected officials have
come to see the irony of past debates about crime. Newark Mayor
Kenneth Gibson has noted, "The same people who used to campaign
against strong law and order measures, perceiving them as a racial
thing, now are actively petitioning City Hall for more police protection and stiffer penalties" (in Cronin et al., 1981: 119). As long as "law
and order" was associated with the "racial thing" and issues such as
lifestyle and public order, those who claimed to speak for the lower
classes could not use the issue of crime (Jacob and Lineberry,
1982a).

Changing the political scenario in which crime is debated by
no means guarantees the formation of effective anti-crime policy.
Reducing crime is difficult. "Root causes" do not seem amenable to

e will be reduced
ding more and bigger
erry, 1981). The aging
d more of an impact on the
rnment programs (Blumstein,

for combatting crime seem to involve
e criminal justice process, working with
embers of their own communities (Muray,
erman, 1983; Merry, 1981). James Q. Wilson
g argue for programs that involve creating more
etween the police and law-abiding citizens in high-
(Wilson and Kelling, 1982). Another leading authority
can policing has gone so far as to argue that the police should
mmunity organizing as one of their prime responsibilities
erman, 1983). The poor and members of minority groups—the
most likely victims of crime—have proven, however, to be the hardest
to mobilize and involve in the criminal justice process (Greenberg et
al., 1984). Although the interests of these groups would be served by
real reductions in crime, they have had good reasons to suspect the
intent of those who traditionally advocated "law and order."

Equality has, however, proven to be a powerful symbol in American
politics. The demand for crime control could be posed as a demand
for social justice. An alternative political scenario could unite traditional liberal ideas about equality with the real need people have to be
protected. Like other public services, protection from crime could be
debated as a public good to which all citizens ought to have an equal
claim. There is no evidence that this kind of demand would be incom-
patible with protecting the rights of the accused. A movement to bring
about equal protection from crime should be appealing to those
interested in reducing crime.

Changing the terms of debate about crime offers no solution to the
problem of crime. However, debating the crime issue in terms of how
to deliver criminal justice services equally and effectively may make
development and implementation of programs that reduce crime
easier.

REFERENCES

ANTON, T. and B. BOWEN (1976) "Toward a clarification of citizen satisfaction
with metropolitan public services." Presented at the American Political Science
Association Convention, Chicago.

BAKER, L. (1983) Miranda. New York: Atheneum.

BENNETT, L. (1975) "Political scenario and the growth of politics." Philosophy and Rhetoric, 8, 1: 23-25.

——— (n.d.) "The symbolic basis of political order." (unpublished)

BLUMSTEIN, A. (1983) "Prisons: population, capacity, and alternatives," in J. Q. Wilson (ed.) Crime and Public Policy. San Francisco: Institute for Contemporary Studies.

BROWN, C. (1972) "Treat this problem like a war effort." New York Times Magazine (September): 95-96.

BURNHAM, D. (1974) "Most call crime cities' worst ill." New York Times (January 16): 1, col. 2-3.

CAMPBELL, A., P. CONVERSE, and W. ROGERS (1976) The Quality of American Life. New York: Russell Sage.

CARRINGTON, F. (1975) The Victims. New Rochelle, NY: 35-39 Arlington House.

CARSON, W. C. (1974) "Symbolic and instrumental dimensions of early factory legislation," in R. Hood (ed.) Crime and Public Policy. New York: Free Press.

CLARK, R. (1970) Crime in America. New York: Simon and Schuster.

CRONIN, T., T. CRONIN, and M. MILAKOVICH (1981) Crime in the Streets. Bloomington: University of Indiana Press.

CROSBY, R. and D. SNYDER (1974) "Crime, victimization, and the black community," in I. Draphin and E. Viano (eds.) Victimology. Lexington, MA: Lexington.

ERIKSON, K. (1966) Wayward Puritans. New York: John Wiley.

FORST, B. (1983) "Prosecution and Sentencing," in J. Q. Wilson (ed.) Crime and Public Policy. San Francisco: I.C.S. Press.

FOWLER, F. (1974) Citizen Attitudes Toward Local Governments, Services and Taxes. Cambridge, MA: Ballinger.

GREEN, E. (1961) Judicial Attitudes in Sentencing. London: Macmillan.

GREENBERG, S., W. ROHE, and J. WILLIAMS (1984) "Informal citizen action and crime prevention at the neighborhood level." Final Report: Executive Summary. Research Triangle, NC: Research Triangle Institute.

GURR, T. R. (1982) "Historical trends in crime: A critical review of the evidence," in M. Tonry and N. Morris, Crime and Justice, 3. Chicago: University of Chicago Press.

GUSFIELD, J. (1963) The Symbolic Crusade. Urbana: University of Illinois Press.

HARLAN, J. (1968) in Duncan v. Louisiana, 391 U.S. 145.

HARRIS, R. (1970) Justice. New York: E.P. Dutton.

HIRSCH, T. (1983) "Crime and the family," in J. Q. Wilson (ed.) Crime and Public Policy. San Francisco: Institute for Contemporary Studies.

HOFSTADTER, R. (1955) Age of Reform. New York: Alfred A. Knopf.

JACOB, H. (1972) "Contact with government agencies: a preliminary analysis of the distribution of urban services." Midwest Journal of Political Science 16: 123.

——— (1971) "Black and white perceptions of law enforcement." Law and Society Review 6: 1:69.

——— and R. LINEBERRY (1982a) Government Responses to Crime: Crime on Urban Agendas. Washington, DC: Government Printing Office.

——— (1982b) Government Responses to Crime: Executive Summary. Washington, DC: Government Printing Office.

——— (1982c) Government Responses to Crime: Crime and Governmental Responses in American Cities. Washington, DC: Government Printing Office.

LINDERSMITH, A. and Y. LEVIN (1937) "The Lombrosian myth in criminology." American Journal of Sociology 42: 5:670.

LOWI, T. (1979) The End of Liberalism. New York: W.W. Norton.

——— (1972) "Four systems of policy, politics and choice." Public Administration Review 34, 4: 298-310.

——— (1970) "Policy making: Toward an antidote for technocracy." Public Administration Review 30, 3: 314-325.

——— (1964) "American business and public policy: case studies and political theory." World Politics 26: 4: 677.

MERRY, S. (1981) Urban Danger. Philadelphia: Temple University Press.

MURAY, C. (1983) "The physical environment and community control of crime," in J. Q. Wilson (ed.) Crime and Public Policy. San Francisco: Institute for Contemporary Studies.

PLATT, A. (1981) "Street crime," in A. Platt and P. Takagi (eds.) Crime and Social Justice. Totowa, NJ: Barnes and Noble.

President's Commission on Law Enforcement and Administration of Justice (1968) The Challenge of Crime in a Free Society. New York: Avon Books.

REIMAN, J. (1979) The Rich Get Richer and the Poor Get Poorer. New York: John Wiley.

RHODES, R. (1977) The Insoluble Problem of Crime. New York: John Wiley.

RUMBLE, W. (1968) American Legal Realism. Ithaca, NY: Cornell University Press.

RYAN, W. (1976) Blaming the Victim. New York: Basic Books.

SAUNDERS, L. (1976) "Effective control of urban crime: mission impossible?" The Crisis: A Record of the Darker Races 5 (May): 157.

SCAMMON, R. and B. WATTENBERG (1970) The Real Majority. New York: Coward-McCann.

SCHEINGOLD, S. (1983) The Politics of Law and Order. New York: Longman.

SCHUR, E. (1969) Our Criminal Society. Englewood Cliffs, NJ: Prentice-Hall.

SHERMAN, L. (1983) "Patrol strategies for police," in J. Q. Wilson (ed.) Crime and Public Policy. San Francisco: Institute for Contemporary Studies.

SKOGAN, W. and M. MAXFIELD (1981) Coping with Crime. Beverly Hills, CA: Sage.

SOLOMAN, F. et al. (1980) "Civil rights activity and reduction in crime among Negroes." Crime and Social Justice 14 (Winter): 27.

STOLZ, B. (1983) "Congress and capital punishment." Law and Policy Quarterly 5, 2: 163.

U.S. Department of Justice (1976) Criminal Victimization in the United States. Washington, DC: Government Printing Office.

WILSON, J. Q. [ed.] (1983) Crime and Public Policy. San Francisco: Institute for Contemporary Studies.

——— (1975) Thinking About Crime. New York: Basic Books.

——— and G. KELLING (1982) "Broken windows." Atlantic Monthly 249 (March): 29-38.

ZEISEL, H. (1982) The Limits of Law Enforcement. Chicago: University of Chicago Press.

II.

*Legislative Politics and the
Criminal Law*

2.

CRIMINAL CODE REFORM AND THE INTEREST GROUP POLITICS OF THE AMERICAN BAR ASSOCIATION

Albert P. Melone
Southern Illinois University at Carbondale

Despite considerable scholarly attention directed toward criminal justice over the last two decades, relatively little literature is available that investigates the legislative roles of interest groups in the enactment of criminal laws (Fairchild, 1981). This is the case for both divisions of the federal system but especially at the national level. A previous study identified twelve groups, including the American Bar Association (ABA), that recurrently appeared before the Senate Judiciary Committee during the 1970s offering testimony on various ill-fated legislative proposals to reform the U.S. Criminal Code (Melone and Slagter, 1983). Although useful in identifying what might be stipulated as a working criminal justice elite, the study did not offer sufficient insight into the dynamics of criminal law policy-making. This chapter is an attempt to remedy the shortcoming by concentrating on a particular interest group.

In general, seminal thinkers such as Weber (in Gerth and Mills, 1946: 85), Durkheim (1958: 7-8), and Tocqueville (1945: 275-276), admonish their readers to ponder the crucial or strategic position enjoyed by attorneys in the making of public policy. Lawyer ubiquity in positions of political prominence is well documented, and conventional wisdom supports the widespread observation that lawyers exercise considerable influence in a variety of policymaking settings. In addition to generalized lawyer influence, the ABA is the foremost nationwide attorney organization possessing high status, effective organization, and skilled leadership. Together these salient characteristics establish the necessary preconditions for an influential or powerful interest group. Besides illustrating how status, organization, and leadership were employed, a case will be made that in fact the association was able to achieve many of its criminal code policy goals.

The basic data for this chapter were gathered in the same manner as the earlier macro-focused study (Melone and Slagter, 1983: 44-45). This involved a careful analysis of the testimony offered by the ABA during Senate Judiciary Committee hearings on the Brown Commission Report (1971), S. 1 (1973), S. 1400 (1973), S. 1 (1975), S. 1437 (1977), S. 1722 (1979), and S. 1723 (1979). Because official printed congressional hearings are not uniformly available, testimony on code reform proposals introduced since 1979 is not analyzed. In any event, sufficient information is available for the 1970s to discover patterns and to adduce generalizations. The *American Bar Association Reports* and other association publications are also referenced to analyze internal group politics and other interactions.

POLICY AND ACCESS

Ordinarily, crime brings to mind murder, rape, robbery, and other violent behavior, but the regulation of business activity deemed antisocial may be processed through the criminal justice system as well. Because a criminal code is a massive document, most interested parties probably would concern themselves with a few selected provisions. However, the ABA is no ordinary interest group. From the initial congressional testimony on code revision in 1971 to its final testimony in 1979, association representatives testified on a wide range of controversial provisions.

As might be expected, the ABA testified on such recognizable criminal code matters as criminal sentencing, probation, insanity defenses, the death penalty, and bail jumping. Yet its testimony went far beyond those aspects of criminal law that typically affect low-status criminal offenders. In fact, it was not the ABA's Section on Criminal Law that offered initial testimony before the Senate Judiciary Committee on code reform. Rather, business-oriented sections were the first to offer congressional testimony, and, indeed, these business-oriented sections offered repeated testimony over the years.

Representatives of the Section on Corporation, Banking and Business Law, the Section on Taxation, and later the Section on Antitrust gave extensive, detailed, well-researched, and cogent criticisms of various code proposals. Representatives from the Criminal Law Section and Section on Criminal Justice also gave extensive testimony. Yet the testimony of the criminal law experts—though well researched and well presented—consumed a smaller fraction of testimony than that presented by the business-oriented sections.

Responding to specific problems, Congress wrote the criminal law in piecemeal fashion. This ad hoc approach to the Criminal Code has led to inconsistency, ambiguity, obsoleteness, and confusing laws and criminal procedures. To remedy these problems, Congress established the Commission on Reform of the Federal Criminal Code in 1966. The commission was headed by former California Governor Edmund G. (Pat) Brown and was composed of members of the House of Representatives, the U.S. Senate, and distinguished judges and attorneys. A fourteen-member advisory committee chaired by former United States Supreme Court Associate Justice Tom C. Clark assisted the commission. In addition, the commission had a highly competent professional staff. After four years of toil, the commission submitted its report to President Nixon in 1971, who hailed the report as a "broad comprehensive framework in which to decide the issues involved in reform of the Federal Criminal Code" (U.S. Congress, Senate, 1971: 5).

Governor Brown and the Senate Judiciary Committee leadership viewed the commission's report in the same light as President Nixon did. They insisted that the report must be treated as a working proposal and not as an unalterable document (USCS, 1971: 2, 15, 96). Yet reform proponents maintained that the Brown Report contained four essential features that should be maintained. Senator John McClellan, former Brown Commission member and chairman of the Senate Judiciary Committee, insisted that the rejection of any one of the four essential features would require a wholesale rewriting of the Brown reform proposal (USCS, 1971: 34). Two of the four features—or premises, as Senator McClellan termed them—were immediately controversial; indeed, subsequent bills modified or dropped the Brown Commission's recommendations on the treatment of federal jurisdiction and on the technique of grading. Subsequent bills introduced in Congress between 1973 and 1979 may be viewed as responses to interest group criticism first heard with respect to the Brown Report.

From the outset, the ABA was actively interested and involved in the Brown Report and subsequent legislative proposals. There are four manifestations of this interest and involvement that merit attention. First, the staff director of the Brown Commission was assisted by Richard A. Green, project director of the ABA Standards of Criminal Justice. Second, when the Brown Commission published its study draft of its proposed code in June, 1970, the ABA Section on Criminal Law appointed three ad hoc committees to analyze the three major divisions of the study. Thus, one year before the commission made its final report a section of the association was busily studying the proposal. There are two other significant points. These ad hoc ABA committees were linked with decision-making centers of power. The ABA Section on Criminal Law reported to the association that it had established a working relationship with the U.S. Department of Justice and with the staff of the Senate Judiciary Committee (ABA, 1972: 786). Finally, at its 1971 annual meeting, the ABA House of Delegates gave its endorsement to the principles underlying the Brown Commission Report. It declared that the report should serve as a working basis for legislative restructuring of the criminal code. Additionally, in 1971 the House of Delegates authorized the Section on Criminal Law to assist the executive and legislative branches of government to develop specific code reform legislation and to coordinate the assistance of those other ABA sections interested in code reform. The procedure essentially required that advanced copies of testimony be circulated to association officers and to the chairmen of the sections of the association having an interest in criminal code reform (ABA, 1972: 520-523).

High Status and Group Effectiveness

ABA recommendations are undoubtedly treated by legislative actors with extraordinary deference. The fact is that ABA representatives are high-status lawyers often having high-status individuals and organizations for clients. Many leaders, defined as members of the ABA's Board of Governors and House of Delegates, are associated with large private law firms with some of the most successful business enterprises in America for clients. For example, in 1975, 60 percent of ABA leaders were associated with firms as large as 9 or more (Melone, 1983: 695) as compared to about 50 percent of all lawyers who are individual practitioners (Curran, 1983: 4). Most of these ABA leaders list corporation or corporate finance law among their specialties, and less than 2 percent of them list criminal law, family law, debt collection, or other low-status specializations. Those leaders had a significant 34 percent of *Fortune Magazine*'s top 500 industrial corporations for clients (Melone, 1983: 694-695). The association's high status is also a result of its performance over the years as an organization that is well prepared and extremely helpful to the Congress. Consider one such example.

Professor Emeritus Livingston Hall of the Harvard Law School and chairman of the ABA Committee on Reform of the Federal Criminal Law gave extensive testimony on its November 1972 written statement. He concentrated on the association's views of appellate review of sentences and how S. 1 should be made to conform to existing ABA standards (USCS, 1973a: 5364-5373). On June 12, 1973, this same ABA spokesman offered testimony on 21 distinct and parallel aspects of S. 1 and S. 1400.

On such diverse issues ranging from federal jurisdiction to the definition of conspiracy (USCS, 1973c: 5818-5825), an examination of Professor Hall's testimony reveals that ABA recommendations were accepted on 40.5 percent of the provisions found in the two bills, partially accepted in 11.9 percent of the cases, and rejected or not followed in 47.6 percent of the provisions. These figures would be more meaningful if they could be compared with success rates of other interest groups. Nevertheless, the ABA clearly does keep score. As Hall put it in his concluding remarks: "Our committee believes that its work . . . was well worth the time and effort that it spent, because we are very pleased to see that a substantial number of our recommendations have been adopted in both bills" (USCS, 1973c: 5825). Members of Congress also viewed ABA approval as desirable. Senator Roman Hruska (R-Neb.), co-sponsor of S. 1 and ranking minority member of the Senate subcommittee holding hearings on S. 1 and S. 1400, said to Professor Hall, "We are gratified at the number of instances when we conform to your recommendations of today. We will take under advisement those instances where we have not conformed" (USCS, 1973c: 5825).

Organization and Group Effectiveness

The ABA is organized in such a fashion that it can muster with relative ease outstanding expert opinion on a wide variety of criminal law topics. Subject specialists in antitrust, taxation, corporation, business, banking, and international law, as well as criminal law and criminal justice studied and made carefully worded recommendations to Congress on code revision. This was possible because the association is organized in part around standing committees called sections. The sections conduct meetings and study laws of interest, and a number have their own journals. Consequently, subject specialists come together regularly to communicate with one another and to offer recommendations on changes in the law that the association as a body should endorse. In the case of criminal code revision, recommendations were often sifted through ad hoc and standing committees, then further discussed and debated in section councils, and, on occasion, debated and amended again by the House of Delegates, the ABA's chief policymaking body. Given the expertise available through its organizational structure, it is little wonder that ABA recommendations were treated with great respect. Consider two examples of the results of this organization. One such instance is provided by Mac Asbill, Jr., chairman of the 14,000-member ABA Section on Taxation. His testimony illustrates how subject experts are capable of raising difficult questions, making others seem less than fully competent.

The Brown proposed code would have shifted some tax crimes from the Internal Revenue Code to Title 18, the Criminal Code. According to Asbill, what would happen to those existing tax crimes not so shifted was not clear. For example, what would happen to Section 7203 relating to the willful failure to pay, keep records, or supply information? Would those provisions be repealed or would they remain as law under Title 26—the Tax Code? Until a satisfactory answer to this question was given, it would be impossible, argued Asbill, to ascertain whether the proposed new code would create gaps or inconsistent and overlapping provisions in the law (USCS, 1972: 1679).

His initial point was one of draftsmanship. However, Asbill went on to argue that, whether intentional or not, many changes in the tax law were included in the proposed code and that the Congress should be fully aware of such changes (USCS, 1972: 1682).

Asbill questioned the Brown Commission's clarity of thought because it dropped deficiency as a requirement for criminal liability. Currently, a substantial deficiency due to fraud must exist in order for a person to be found guilty of tax evasion, but deficiency need not be a required element under the proposed code. Thus a person might be branded a tax evader if, in fact, he evaded no tax and reported the amount of tax actually due. This paradox arose because presently the willful filing of a tax return that is known to be false as to a material matter, though it is not tax evasion, is a felony even if no tax is owed. Under the Brown recommendations that offense, absent a deficiency, would become a Class A misdemeanor. This would have been true because under the proposed code a deficiency must be present for felony treatment. In rhetorical fashion Asbill asked whether the downgrading of the offense was really intended. He went on to question other provisions, raising similar queries about unintended consequences (USCS, 1972: 1683-1684) and, by implication, the thoughtfulness of the Brown Report itself.

Testimony was not limited to pointing out unintended consequences. At one point Asbill raised a question of elementary logic. The Internal Revenue Code provided that all tax evasions are felonies, subject to the requirement of a substantial deficiency due to fraud. However, the proposed code would grade the crime of tax evasion according to the size of the deficiency. So, for example, if the tax deficiency exceeds $500, the crime is a felony; if the deficiency is $500 or less, the crime is a misdemeanor. Yet the exact amount of the tax deficiency in most instances cannot be known until the facts are established in court. Consequently, no one can know whether the crime would be a felony or a misdemeanor until the trial is complete and the amount of the tax deficiency is, as a matter of law, determined (USCS, 1972: 1685). This logical difficulty in turn raises at least 3 serious procedural problems. First, should the government prosecutor proceed by way of information or indictment? Second, how many challenges is each party entitled to during the course of empaneling a jury? Finally, there would be no prior way to know which statute of limitations is applicable because, under the Brown proposal, the limitation period would be 3 years for a misdemeanor and 5 years for a felony (USCS, 1972: 1685).

At least seven other features of the proposed code were assailed further by Asbill. He concluded in a manner typical of ABA representatives. The ABA tax expert testified that his section was anxious to work on the inside of the legislative system. Asbill said, "We would consider it a privilege to be called upon to assist the subcommittee [Criminal Laws and Procedure of the Committee of the Judiciary] and its staff in completing the job" (USCS, 1972: 1702). This legislative strategy was repeated many times. Through careful study and documentation, the ABA puts itself in the position of expert advisor. Through making itself available to the Congress for further consultation, it puts itself in a position to shape final policy outcomes to its liking.

A second example of the functionality of the ABA's organizational structure is provided by testimony on two bills considered in 1979. The ABA was represented at the Senate hearings by Professor William Greenhalgh, chairman of the Criminal Justice Section's Criminal Revision Committee; George C. Freeman, Jr., chairman of the ABA Corporation, Banking and Business Law Section ad hoc committee on Federal Criminal Code Reform; and Laurie Robinson, director of the ABA's Section on Criminal Justice. Together they suggested that the Senate Judiciary Committee "consider the possibility of using our [ABA] good offices as an independent group to resolve presently existing differences between S. 1722 and S. 1723 [the House bill]" (USCS, 1979: 9967). The clear implication is that the ABA, which believes in code reform and is widely respected for its sincerity, expert knowledge, and objectivity, should be called upon to play the role of honest broker. Why not? After all, as association leaders have argued, the ABA possesses expert knowledge and is apparently respected by key decision makers for its selfless pursuit of the public interest (Melone, 1977: 15-16).

For a group to assume such a public posture requires that it possess internal group cohesion. Yet the ABA was not always united on all aspects of proposed code reform. The comments of Freeman both substantiate this observation and illustrate the importance group leaders attribute to a public presentation of internal group cohesion. Freeman remarked (USCS, 1979: 9969):

> I would like to say I don't want Bill's [William Greenhalgh's] introductory remarks to leave you with the impression that the American Bar Association is still internally generally divided amongst the resolutions which have been adopted by the House of Delegates and the positions which are reflected in our testimony.

> I would say that 95 or 98 percent of those resolutions were unanimously supported by all the interested sections and unanimously adopted by the ABA House of Delegates.

> In the areas where we had differences of view, largely with regard to sanctions for organizations and appellate review of sentences at the instances of the government, in those areas we have through further discussions considerably narrowed the differences within the association.

> I am pleased to report to you that the revised criminal standard on organizational sanctions adopted by the House of Delegates was unanimously sponsored by representatives of the standing committee on standards of criminal justice, the sections of corporation, banking, and business law, antitrust and the representatives of the criminal justice section participated in the discussions preceding that resolution and was unanimously adopted by the House of Delegates.

> I would also say that on the appeal of sentences, we have been given instructions by the ABA not to take any position for or against government appeal of sentence while the matter is under reconsideration by the ABA. We hope to be able to come back to you with an association position on that in the near future.

Thus Freeman assured the Senate Committee that although expert ABA opinion may have at one time been somewhat divided, the association now stood united on almost every matter affecting criminal code revision. In other words, the policy cues were clear and unequivocal. If only legislators would adopt ABA recommendations, this line of reasoning went, the criminal code controversy could come to a happy conclusion. The experts had employed their specialized legal skills to aid in drafting reasonable legislation; now it was time for the political decision makers to permit lawyers to employ their broader political skills as honest brokers of political conflict.

Political Skills

High status and effective organization, though necessary, are not sufficient conditions for converting political demands into policy outcomes. Leadership must be schooled sufficiently in the art of interest group politics so as to know which conduct is likely to produce desired results. The political skills displayed by the ABA leadership are exemplary.

Association spokespersons who testified before congressional committees were most often not specifically authorized to represent their own views as those of the association. Nonetheless, they were placed in a position to influence legislation. This was accomplished by affording association representatives an opportunity to present testimony in person or in writing on every criminal code reform bill even though the House of Delegates did not pass specific resolutions authorizing particular policy stands. Thus without inflicting undue internal disunity, the association was able to present a public presence.

ABA representatives certainly did not give the impression that they were hired guns for special interests. Rather, in a most skillful if not unique rhetorical fashion, ABA representatives presented and were received as impartial experts aiding the Congress in obtaining a worthy goal. This posture was possible given the cultural responsiveness to legal symbols. ABA recommendations are regarded as the voice of nonpartisanship and value objective reason. Legalism as an ideology places the ABA above politics, yet simultaneously in the midst of the political thicket. Therefore, the question of whose ox is being gored is easily deflected by appeals to the rule of law.

A vivid example of this view is provided by Donald McDonald, chairman of the Section on Taxation. During his presentation of the section's criticisms on S. 1 (1973) and S. 1400 (1973), he asserted:

> While the Section is composed principally of private practitioners, we have avoided a defense counsel orientation. Our professional responsibility and representation, encompassing, as it does, federal taxation, concerns laws to which virtually every citizen is subject. Thus, perhaps uniquely in our field, "justice to the individual and justice to the society as a whole are one and the same interest" (USCS, 1973b: 5629).

This happy self-concept does not necessarily nor easily translate into universally discernible self-evident truths. After all, bill authors proposed changes in the tax law that were disagreeable to the taxation section. Yet this expression of the selfless pursuit of justice is probably not a deliberate sham. The confusion of value preferences for actual behavior is a common human misunderstanding.

Evidence of personal interaction also exists among ABA subject specialists and Senate Judiciary Committee staff persons and other government officials. For example, signaling a working relationship with the Senate staff, Donald McDonald noted that he had the "privilege of conferring with Mr. G. Robert Blakey and other members of the Staff . . . and have only praise for the high degree of care, competence, and concern of those working on the Project" (USCS, 1973b: 5629). McDonald also revealed an ABA/Justice Department communication dyad when, in an exchange with Blakey about a disputed provision of the proposed legislation, he said, "We still prefer, particularly in light of the Department of Justice's concessions in discussions with us that they do not prosecute unless there is a substantial deficiency" (USCS, 1973b: 5644).

An article first appearing in the ABA's *Antitrust Law Journal* and later inserted in the Senate hearings illustrates yet another aspect of the ABA's political sophistication (USCS, 1974b: 8133-8178). It is a reproduction of the proceedings of a panel meeting that convened at the antitrust law section's annual spring meeting on April 4-5, 1974. It underscores the access and interaction of the private bar, government officials, and key congressional staff.

Panel participants included Mark Crane, chief spokesman for the antitrust law section before the Senate Judiciary Committee; George W. Liebmann, a private member of the Illinois and Maryland bars and a section member; James T. Halverson, director, Bureau of Competition, Federal Trade Commission (FTC); and Paul C. Summitt, chief counsel, Senate Judiciary Subcommittee on Criminal Laws and Procedures. The panel was chaired by Denis G. McInerney, chairman, Criminal Practice and Procedure Committee of the Antitrust Section. The two section members, Crane and Liebmann, presented essentially the same comments as were presented before the Senate subcommittee in 1973. The section leadership was able in this way to disseminate its views to section members receiving and reading the *Journal*, a classic example of an active minority informing and educating the members of an organization on the salient issues of the day.

Halverson of the Federal Trade Commission presented his views expressing opposition to some provisions and declaring support for other S. 1 and S. 1400 sections.

Bringing FTC staff personnel together with antitrust section members is not uncommon. Between 1968 and 1980, 10.2 percent of ABA Antitrust Section officers and council members were at one time or another during their professional careers associated with the FTC. During this same period, FTC officials participated in ABA antitrust section meetings an average of 3.6 times per year (Melone, 1983: 692-693). Clearly, the ABA enjoys open communication with the government regulators. To the extent that it can influence FTC thinking, the association is that much more influential.

The presentation by Paul C. Summitt of the Senate Judiciary Committee illustrates not only the access to centers of political power enjoyed by the ABA but also the deference afforded the association among governmental functionaries. Summitt first stated "the main function [of the panel] is to educate me, rather than for me to try to educate you. You already know the field" (USCS, 1974b: 8170). Summitt described the history of Senate staff involvement in code revision and answered some questions concerning the legislation. The friendly first-name basis of the panel discussion ended with Summitt inviting letters from interested members of the audience to the Senate Judiciary Committee (USCS, 1974b: 8178).

Another example of the use of in-house ABA publications for political purposes is provided by Charles S. Maddock of the ABA Section on Corporation, Banking, and Business Law. He was not satisfied to rest his case before the Senate subcommittee with appearances in two consecutive years, so he penned an article entitled, "The Proposed Criminal Code: Business Lawyer Beware." This piece appeared in the April, 1974 issue of *The Business Lawyer*, an official organ of the ABA Section on Corporation, Banking, and Business Law. The journal editor signaled to the specialist audience the importance of code reform. He wrote, "The position as lead article of Mr. Maddock's observations indicates the importance that the editors ascribe to the issues it raises for all business lawyers and corporate executives" (USCS, 1974a: 7517).

The article itself repeats essentially the arguments made during congressional testimony. ABA leaders were fully cognizant of how to use the in-house publications to generate both internal group cohesion and additional support for its policy objectives. The article was an unequivocal call to arms beseeching business lawyers to make themselves familiar with the terms of the proposed code and to become actively involved in making their feelings known within existing bar and trade associations or do so individually (USCS, 1974a: 7527-7528). A reprint of the Maddock article was submitted for the record to the Senate subcommittee. It provided the political information to members of the Senate that business lawyers and executives have been apprised of the section's policy recommendations. In brief, Maddock presented the party line to the membership. The members were asked to join with the leadership in placing demands upon the political system. The relevant political actors were then given this important political intelligence to consider in their own decision-making calculus. Such tactics are well-known. That the ABA employs such tools speaks eloquently about the leadership's understanding of interest group politics.

INFLUENCE

Based upon what has already been documented, clearly the ABA evidences high status, effective organization, and exemplary political skills. Deducing political influence from the existence of these vital characteristics is not, however, the same as demonstrating such influence. Preferably influence is demonstrated in its own right, independent of the strong evidence that conditions existed to make the ABA a powerful force in code revision. Nonetheless, demonstrating an empirical linkage is difficult for at least two reasons. First, no objective criteria exist for judging the efforts of interest groups. In other words, what are the bench marks for success? Is getting no bill passed better than having one enacted that contains objectionable features? Should a relatively few number of bill provisions favored by a group be singled out to determine if those provisions were written into a bill, and if so, how should those of "lesser importance" be weighted? Second, the matter of influence is relative. By what other interest group or institution should the ABA's success rate be judged? This matter is made even more complicated by the fact that, in the case of code reform, no two interest groups testified on the same number of identical provisions found in each proposed bill. The lack of testimony on parallel provisions renders impossible comparative analysis of group rates except in the crudest fashion.

The above caveats notwithstanding, a conclusion that the ABA was influential in the code reform debate of the 1970s seems reasonable. There are four points considered together that lead to this conclusion. Some have already been mentioned but bear repeating in this context whereas others provide additional empirical evidence.

First, for a group to possess influence it must participate in the policymaking process. In systemic terms, groups must first place demands upon the system before those demands can be converted into policy outcomes. The ABA fulfilled this threshold requirement. It offered testimony at congressional hearings on all bills considered by the Senate on criminal code revision during the 1970s. As previously noted, the project director of the ABA Standards on Criminal Justice assisted the staff director of the Brown Commission, the body that took four years to study code revision and produced the initial proposal that provided the basis for much of the revision debate throughout the decade. The association formed special ad hoc committees to study code reform, and it permitted section representatives to testify before congressional committees. In addition to those sections specializing in criminal law and criminal justice, subject specialists in business law, taxation, antitrust, and international law made congressional appearances, and most followed up their initial testimony with letters, documents, and additional testimony in person on successor bills. Moreover, through the use of in-house publication organs, the association reached lawyers around the country admonishing them to make their individual views known to policymakers.

The acknowledgment by decision makers of interest group contributions to the policymaking process is evidence of likely group influence, though not a necessary condition for its existence. As such, it is a second point to be considered when ascertaining ABA influence. Senators and staff personnel on repeated occasions thanked ABA representatives for their carefully studied recommendations. Senator Edward M. Kennedy (D-Mass.), chairman of the Judiciary Committee, writing in that committee's reports to the Senate on S. 1437 (1977) and S. 1722 (1979), named ten organizations as providing great amounts of study, discussion, and preparation helpful to the committee in its work. He specifically named the ABA's sections on Taxation, Antitrust, Corporation, Banking and Business Law, and Criminal Law (USCS, 1977: 13-14; USCS, 1980: 14).[1] Thus, once again but in a different context, ABA contributions to code revision were acknowledged by a political actor in a position to know.

The third and fourth points are best considered together. The third concerns the belief or self-perception of having influence. Probably a person who expresses feelings of efficacy is in possession of at least some degree of influence. Of course, depending upon circumstances, political actors have been known to feign both power and powerlessness. Sometimes honest self-assessments of power relationships are erroneously evaluated. That is why, when possible, ascertainment of influence independent of self-descriptions or retrospective interviews is preferable. Thus the fourth and last point suggesting influence is the actual extent to which ABA policy recommendations were adopted. Considered together, points three and four seem persuasive.

Charles S. Maddock of the ABA Section on Corporation, Banking, and Business Law appeared twice before the Senate subcommittee (USCS, 1972: 1642-1649; USCS, 1973d: 6652-6661). The second time, he spent some time comparing S. 1 (1973) and S. 1400 (1973) with his earlier recommendations on the Brown Report (1971).

The testimony reveals that about half of the objectionable Brown Report features were remedied in S. 1. Those satisfactory provisions included organizational criminal liability, personal criminal liability for conduct on behalf of organizations, the definition of organization, and the interference with activities of employees and employers. However, S. 1 provisions dealing with special sanctions for organizations, disqualification from organizational functions, regulatory offenses, and securities violations remained unsatisfactory as they were in the Brown Report. The only satisfactory provision in S. 1400 was that relating to regulatory offenses. This is so because, in this instance, the bill did not provide for such offenses.

At least for the case of S. 1, the Maddock recommendations probably had some impact on the Senate leadership responsible for the bill's formulation. The Maddock testimony alone, however, did not cause the favorable changes from the Brown recommendations. On the other hand, Maddock apparently believed that his earlier testimony had some impact because he did say in addressing the Senate subcommittee, "We are very pleased to find that many of the objections that our section had to the final report of the Brown Commission have been answered in comparable provisions of Senate Bill No. 1" (USCS, 1973d: 6653). Causation and certainly single causes are most difficult to prove in any science. However, a necessary condition for a "causal relationship" is present; ABA testimony is followed by ABA recommended changes.

Also scrutinize the written testimony submitted on S. 1 (USCS, 1975) from Mark Crane of the ABA's Criminal Practice and Procedure Committee of the Antitrust Section. Crane first thanked the Senate subcommittee and its staff for the opportunity two years earlier to present the views of his antitrust committee on the ill-fated S. 1 (USCS, 1973) and S. 1400 (USCS, 1973) bills. He then went on to state, "We are pleased that the present version of S. 1 incorporates most of the changes we suggested, and we, of course, reaffirm our support of those changes. This leaves only three provisions on which we wish to comment with respect to the present bill" (USCS, 1975: 233). Crane had reason to feel efficacious; comparing his 1973 testimony to the present, over 80 percent of his objections were met in S. 1 (USCS, 1975). Of course, a note of caution should be sounded. Testimony on an earlier bill cannot with certitude be considered to cause changes in future bills. At the least, though, Crane and his committee can claim probable impact. This may be warranted because he was the only person back in 1973 to offer specific testimony against S. 1 and S. 1400 provisions affecting antitrust laws.

The evidence of ABA influence is not all positive. Indeed, a case can be made that ABA fortunes were inconsistent. First ponder the association's success record with respect to S. 1437 (USCS, 1977) provisions.

When comparing ABA policies to the provisions of S. 1437, clearly the bill contained, from an association perspective, many objectionable provisions. Indeed, in testimony 2 years later on a successor bill, an ABA representative submitted for the record an 18-page appendix that, in part, compared ABA policies with S. 1437 provisions (USCS, 1979: 9996-10014). Table 2.1 contains a distillation of the relevant parts of that appendix.

Note at first that the ABA is careful to record which of its policy recommendations are being followed and which are being discarded; once again, a fortiori, it is evident that it "keeps score." Second, of the 54 total subjects mentioned, S. 1437 was fully consistent with ABA policies in 20 instances, consistent if amended in 7 cases, and inconsistent in 25 instances. The association expressed no policy preference in 2 cases. Thus close to half of all ABA policy expressions on criminal code reform were in disagreement with the Senate passed bill.

No objective criteria are available for judging a 50 percent failure rate as good, bad, or indifferent. For one thing, the ABA probably does not consider each policy position to be of equal importance. Thus treating each policy position equally is probably misleading. For example, S. 1437 is consistent with long-held ABA policies concerning liability of an organization, attempt, conspiracy, and solicitation. Yet the association seemed to be back to square one on the salient matters of culpability, liability of an agent for conduct of an organization, and antitrust offense grading. Then, too, after 6 or 7 years of lobbying, the association, if truly influential, should have had a success rate closer to 100 percent.

Although the ABA is a certainly highly visible participant in the policymaking process, the fact is it cannot expect to be completely

TABLE 2.1

ABA Policies Compared to Provisions of S. 1437

Supportive	Supportive with Amendments	Opposed	No Opinion
General Statement of Purposes	Statute of Limitations	Jurisdiction	Obstructing a Government Function by Fraud
Liability of an Organization	Immaturity	Culpability	Modification of Term of Imprisonment
Selective Inclusion of Bars and Defenses	Employment of Illegal Aliens	Complicity, Accessories, and Co-conspirators	
Attempt	Bail Jumping	Liability of an Agent for Conduct of an Organization	
Conspiracy	Restitution	Enforcement of Agency	
Solicitation	Offenders with Mental Disease or Defect	Subpoenas	
Espionage and Related Offenses	Appellate Review of Sentence	False Statements/Records	
Sex Offenses		Reckless Endangerment	
Mail and Other Fraudulent Schemes		Consumer Fraud	
Mandatory Minimum for Firearms Crimes		Antitrust Offense Grading	
Failing to Obey a Public Safety Order		Mandatory Minimum for Drug Offenses	
Crimes in Federal Enclaves		Marijuana Possession	
Presentence Reports		Obscenity	
Imposition of Sentence		Prostitution	
Maximum Terms of Imprisonment		Authorized Sentences	
Post-Release Supervision and Additional Term of Revocation		Notice of Conviction	
Multiple Sentences of Imprisonment		Probation	
Good Time Allowance		Fines	
Crime Victim Compensation		Use Immunity	
Correction or Reduction of Sentence		Pretrial Release	
Child Snatching		Parole Abolition	
		Special Grand Juries	
		Burden of Proof for Affirmative Defenses	
		Procedure Prior to Imposition of Sentence	
		Sentencing Commission	

SOURCE: USCS (1979: 9966-10014).

successful all of the time. Obviously other interests, individuals, institutions, and ideas place conflicting demands upon the political system, tugging and pulling in a variety of directions. That is, after all, an outstanding feature of the special interest process explicit in American pluralism. However, the ABA is not simply one of a number of equally powerful interest groups. It is, to be sure, more equal than most. A more favorable appraisal of its influence can be inferred from the evidence available on the next bill to be considered by the Senate in 1979.

A comparison of 50 parallel provisions of S. 1437 (USCS, 1977) and S. 1722 (USCS, 1979) reveals that although the ABA did not backslide on S. 1437 improvements won in testimony on earlier Senate bills, it was able at the same time to support many S. 1722 changes that it viewed as distinct improvements over the 1977 bill.

Table 2.2 indicates that on balance the ABA viewed S. 1722 (USCS, 1979) as an improvement over S. 1437 (USCS, 1977). Its stance on provisions of the 2 bills changed at an absolute rate of $C = .280$; in 14 of 50 cases (28 percent), the ABA position changed. Of the total amount of change that could have taken place among the 3 support categories, theta (θ) is equal to .223, or over 22 percent. Moreover, as evidenced by the delta statistic ($\Delta = .857$), when the aggregate sum of the changes from support toward opposition categories is subtracted from the sum of the changes from opposition toward support, then clearly the direction of the ABA change in support for the 2 bills was positive and close to perfect.[2] In other words, when the ABA changed its position on various bill provisions, that change was almost always toward support and away from disagreement. Moreover, the content of the proposed legislation was changing, not ABA policy.

In short, many S. 1722 provisions reflected previous ABA recommendations. Also some provisions, though not wholly consistent with association views, displayed movement toward the recommended course. Nonetheless, the ABA failed to get its recommendations accepted in a number of important matters. However, clearly its representatives felt their efforts made a difference. To interpret the evidence otherwise is difficult.

Considering the totality of the circumstances and the relative paucity of evidence to support the null hypothesis, a reasonable conclusion is that the ABA exercised considerable influence in the criminal code revision debate during the 1970s. At the least, the preponderance of the evidence points clearly to such a judgment.

TABLE 2.2
Comparison of ABA Policies on S. 1437 (1977)
and S. 1722 (1979) Provisions

| | S. 1437 | | | |
	Supported	Supported with Amendments	Opposed	Totals
S. 1722				
Support	18 (36%)	0 (0%)	7 (14%)	25 (50%)
Support with Amendments	1 (2%)	6 (12%)	6 (12%)	13 (26%)
Oppose	0 (0%)	0 (0%)	12 (24%)	12 (24%)
Totals	19 (38%)	6 (12%)	25 (50%)	50 (100%)

C = Absolute change = .280
θ = Magnitude of change = .223
Δ = Net direction of the magnitude = .857

CONCLUSION

Private governments possessing high status, effective organization, and skilled leadership are potentially powerful interest groups. The ABA fits the description, and its involvement in criminal code revision illustrates the point.

Reading the testimony of all the groups and individuals offering criminal code recommendations during the 1970s leaves a distinct impression that some groups were better received by the Senate Judiciary Committee than others. Group status is a partial explanation. All Senate Judiciary Committee members are themselves lawyers, and thus ABA representatives are viewed as members of the same professional club. Yet, ABA representatives are not ordinary run-of-the-mill lawyers. By professional success standards, most ABA representatives offering congressional testimony were at the zenith of the stratified bar. Many were private practitioners associated in large law firms with some of the richest corporations in America for clients. A few, such as Livingston Hall of the Harvard Law School, were distinguished scholars. Thus as David Truman (1958: 265) has pointed out, the recommendations of high status groups to government officials may "in some instances appear less as demands of supplications and more as flattery of the official of whom a favor is asked."

In some part, the high status enjoyed by the ABA is due to its effective internal organization and to the outstanding political skills of its leadership. The association's influence is in large part attributable to the possession of these outstanding characteristics.

Future research should investigate the political roles of other interest groups. The National Council on Crime and Delinquency, the American Law Institute, the Federal Public Defenders Association, and the American Civil Liberties Union are just a few that come immediately to mind. Such studies could help to create a deeper understanding of the dynamics underlying criminal justice policy-making.

NOTES

1. The other groups named by Senator Kennedy include: the Association of the Bar of the City of New York, the American Civil Liberties Union, the National Legal Aid and Defender Association, the National Council on Crime and Delinquency, the New York County Lawyers Association, the National District Attorney's Association, the National Association for the Advancement of Colored People Legal Defense and Education Fund, the National Association of Attorneys General, and the Committee for Economic Development (USCS, 1977: 14). Senator Kennedy named these same groups including the American Bar Association when he submitted the Judiciary Committee's report on the *Criminal Code Reform Act* of 1979 (USCS, 1980: 14).

2. Rather than reporting traditional measures of association that convey at best ambiguous information, I have chosen to employ two measures first employed in a 1982 published work (Melone and Jones, 1982: 184-192). Theta (θ) measures the magnitude of change and can be interpreted as the proportion of possible change occurring between $time_1$ and $time_2$, that is, the change in ABA support found in S. 1437 to that found in S. 1722. Delta (Δ) denotes the net direction of that magnitude of change. It reflects the proportion of the positive/negative magnitude of change remaining after a compensatory amount of the opposite magnitude that has also occurred has been cancelled. Theta (θ) ranges from zero (0) to one (1); zero means that no change has occurred; one indicates that all possible change that could have occurred did, in fact, do so. Delta (Δ) varies from $+1$ to -1; zero (0) means that an equal amount of change occurred in both directions, effectively cancelling out movements in each. (For a detailed elaboration of these statistics see: Jones, 1980).

REFERENCES

American Bar Association (1972) Annual Report of the American Bar Association: 1971, 96. Chicago: American Bar Association.

CURRAN, B. A. (1983) "The Legal profession in the 1980s: The changing profile of the legal profession." Presented at a Research Seminar by the Fellows of the American Bar Foundation, Atlanta, Georgia.

DURKHEIM, E. (1958) Professional Ethics and Civil Morals. Glencoe: Free Press.

FAIRCHILD, E. S. (1981) "Interest groups in the criminal justice process." Journal of Criminal Justice 9: 181-194.

GERTH, H. H. and C. W. MILLS (1946) Max Weber: Essays in Sociology. New York: Oxford University Press.

JONES, J. (1980) "Two new measures of changes for panel data: Its magnitude and new direction." Presented at the 1980 Annual Meeting of the American Political Science Association, Washington, D.C.

MELONE, A. P. (1983) "The American Bar Association, antitrust legislation and interest group coalitions." Policy Studies Journal 11 (June): 684-698.

——— (1977) Lawyers, Public Policy and Interest Group Politics. Washington, DC: University Press of America.

——— and J. H. JONES (1982) "Constitutional convention delegates and interest groups: A panel study of elite socialization." Journal of Politics 44 (February): 184-192.

MELONE, A. P. and R. SLAGTER (1983) "Interest group politics and reform of the federal criminal code," In Nagel et al. (eds.) The Political Science of Criminal Justice. Springfield, IL: Charles C Thomas.

TOCQUEVILLE, A. (1945) Democracy in America. New York: Alfred A. Knopf.

TRUMAN, D. B. (1958) The Governmental Process. New York: Alfred A. Knopf.

U.S. Congress, Senate (1980) Criminal Code Reform Act of 1979. S. Rept. 96-553 to accompany S. 1722. 96th Cong., 1st sess.

——— (1979) Committee on the Judiciary. Reform of the Federal Criminal Laws. Hearings Before the Subcommittee on Criminal Laws and Procedures on S. 1722 and S 1723, Part XIV. 96th Cong., 1st sess.

——— (1977) Criminal Code Reform Act of 1977. S. Rept. 95-605 to accompany S. 1437. 94th Cong., 1st sess.

——— (1975) Committee on the Judiciary. The Criminal Justice Reform Act of 1975. Hearings Before the Subcommittee on Criminal Laws and Procedures on S. 1, Part XII. 94th Cong., 1st sess.

——— (1974a) Committee on the Judiciary. Reform of the Federal Criminal Laws. Hearings Before the Subcommittee on Criminal Laws and Procedures on S. 1 and S. 1400, Part X. 93rd Cong., 2nd sess.

——— (1974b) Committee on the Judiciary. Reform of the Federal Criminal Laws. Hearings Before the Subcommittee on Criminal Laws and Procedures on S. 1 and S. 1400, Part XI.

——— (1973a) Committee on the Judiciary. Reform of the Federal Criminal Laws. Hearings Before the Subcommittee on Criminal Laws and Procedures on S. 1, and S. 716, S. 1400 and S. 1401, Part V. 93rd Cong., 1st sess.

——— (1973b) Committee on the Judiciary. Reform of the Federal Criminal Laws. Hearings Before the Subcommittee on Criminal Laws and Procedures on S. 1, S. 716. and S. 1400 and Part IV 93rd Cong., 1st sess.

——— (1973c) Committee of the Judiciary. Reform of the Federal Criminal Laws. Hearings Before the Subcommittee on Criminal Laws and Procedures on S. 1 and S. 1400, Part VII. 93rd Cong., 1st sess.

——— (1973d) Committee of the Judiciary. Reform of the Federal Criminal Laws. Hearings Before the Subcommittee on Criminal Laws and Procedures on S. 1 and S. 1400, Part IX. 93rd Cong., 1st sess.

——— (1972) Committee on the Judiciary. Reform of the Federal Criminal Laws. Hearings Before the Subcommittee on Criminal Laws and Procedures, Part III, Subpart B. 92nd Cong., 2nd sess.

——— (1971) Committee on the Judiciary. Reform of the Federal Criminal Laws. Hearings Before the Subcommittee on Criminal Laws and Procedures, Part I. 92nd Cong., 1st sess.

3.

LEGISLATOR IDEOLOGY AND CRIMINAL JUSTICE POLICY:
Implications from Illinois

Francis T. Cullen
University of Cincinnati

Timothy S. Bynum
University of Maryland

Kim Montgomery Garrett
Louisiana Coalition on Jails and Prisons

Jack R. Greene
Temple University

Since the philosophy of individualized treatment was initially introduced into American corrections during the Progressive era, legislators
have typically imposed only loose constraints on judicial and parole
authorities in the sanctioning of offenders (Rothman, 1980). For the
most part, lawmakers were content to pass criminal codes that carried
stiff maximum sentences—a "loud bark"—but then to allow judges
and parole boards to determine how severe the "bite" or "treatment"
should actually be (Zimring, 1976: 15). Beginning in the mid-1970s,
however, politicians in a number of states moved forcefully to play a
more active role in controlling the fate offenders would be compelled
to endure. Frequently in the name of "law and order" and of purging
leniency from courts that did nothing more than teach the wayward
that crime pays, they sought to fetter severely the discretionary
decision making of judges and parole boards by passing statutes that
mandated prison terms and abolished parole release in favor of determinate sentences. In short, a concerted effort was made by legislators

to effect a fundamental redistribution of power, transferring decision making away from criminal justice participants and to themselves (Dershowitz, 1976: 79). U.S. Representative Sam Steiger (1976: 220, 222) captured the sentiments of many of his brethren when he remarked:

> How often do we read or hear about the crime committed by a person on probation or who has a felony sentence suspended? . . . If the courts are too slow in perceiving the truth of the present situation and continue to be guided by discredited sentiments, I think there is no alternative left to lawmakers but to turn to mandatory penalties . . . I recognize that there are certain problems with shackling the judges in this regard. However, I think the courts have left us no alternative.

This campaign to reshape American criminal justice has been greeted by a flurry of activity assessing its merits. These analyses have generally involved an examination of the specifics of the laws passed and of their ramifications for the system (Blumstein et al., 1983; Casper et al., 1982; Cavender, 1982; Cullen and Gilbert, 1982; Goodstein, 1983; Greenberg and Humphries, 1980; Hussey and Lagoy, 1983; Lagoy, 1981; Lagoy and Kramer, 1980). Curiously, however, these works have tended to share a common omission. Despite the recent efforts of legislators ostensibly aimed at expanding their control within the criminal justice arena, current commentators have been reluctant to investigate systematically what legislators do in fact think about crime and related policy issues. Instead, they often rely, if implicitly, upon the assumption—commonly held by criminologists—that politicians are essentially unenlightened about criminal justice matters and uniformly punitive in their orientation. Mattick's (1976: 294) words, though somewhat marked by hyperbole, are reflective of this viewpoint:

> With a few notable exceptions, legislators . . . are stuck on dead center. . . . The spokesmen, caught up in the froth of a newsworthy current event, pontificate with their fund of eighteenth- and nineteenth-century notions about the treatment of crime and criminals, and the mass media represent these notions to the general public where they are taken as twentieth-century gospel. This completes the cycle of manufacturing the mass delusion that victimizes us all.

Notably, this imagery of legislators contains flaws. At the least, it begs an empirical test. More generally, it ignores the potential complexity of the ideology that prevails in political bodies. As Jacobs (1983: 131) has cautioned, "many commentators seem to think of the legislature as a monolith, a single 'mind set.' Legislators obviously differ substantially on criminal justice matters." Finally, this vision nourishes a pessimistic, if not fully cynical, attitude regarding policy reform: Because few progressive sentiments are present among legislators, American criminal justice is doomed to follow an agenda informed by ignorance and by "get tough" thinking that will do little more than fuel the crisis of escalating prison populations.

In this light, the current study endeavors to assess the criminal justice ideology of one legislative body: Illinois. Through a survey of state senators and representatives, we attempt to measure the nature of the politicians' attitudes toward the origin of crime, policy alternatives, the goals of imprisonment, prison conditions, and rehabilitation. Special attention is given to the extent to which the legislators embrace conservative or liberal stances on these issues. Similar to the limited research conducted previously (Berk and Rossi, 1977; Cullen, Gilbert, and Cullen, 1983), the data revealed considerable ideological diversity among the Illinois lawmakers. The implications of these findings for policymaking and the possibility of future reform efforts are also considered.

METHODS

Sample

In the fall of 1982, questionnaires were sent to all 236 members of the Illinois State Legislature. This study employed the TDM survey technique developed by Dillman (1978), which involved sending a postcard reminder as well as two follow-up questionnaires. In all, 101 usable surveys were returned, a response rate of 42.8 percent. This figure fell far below the 70 percent return typically secured through Dillman's survey method. Furthermore, the failure to obtain a higher level of returns heightens the potential that a response bias characterizes the sample and suggests that the results should be viewed with appropriate caution. At the same time, the present study has the advantage of supplying data on a population that is intimately involved in policymaking yet infrequently researched by criminologists.

There are three factors that may have contributed to the fact that a lower response rate was achieved than in other Dillman surveys.

First, the study was conducted during an election year, which may have placed time constraints on the respondents. Second, the size of the Illinois Legislature was in the process of being reduced markedly. Possibly outgoing politicians may not have seen the relevancy of expressing their opinions in a survey of "legislators." Third, legislators may constitute an inherently difficult population to survey through mailed questionnaires, particularly when the researchers are not direct constituents. Alternatively, a more adequate response rate might be possible when resources permit the scheduling of interviews at the legislators' convenience (Berk and Rossi, 1977: 15-16).

Information on the status characteristics of the responding legislators was obtained. Their mean age was 50.1; 80.2 percent were male and 89.1 percent were white; they averaged 15.7 years of education; and they earned over $40,000 in annual salary. Politically, they had been members of the legislature a mean of 7.8 years. A small majority (54.5 percent) reported that they were Republicans, 44.5 percent said they were Democrats, and only 1 percent claimed to be Independents. In characterizing their political orientation, 1 percent answered extremely liberal, 3.1 percent very liberal, 12.4 percent liberal, 38.1 percent middle of the road, 38.1 percent conservative, 4.1 percent very conservative, and 3.1 percent extremely conservative. Finally, 18.8 percent said that they represented mostly rural jurisdictions, 35.6 percent mostly suburban jurisdictions, and 40.6 percent mostly urban jurisdictions. Taken together, then, the average respondent would be a relatively affluent white male about 50 who is moderate to conservative in political orientation and who has served several terms.

Measures

The questionnaire used in this research contained 64 items assessing attitudes toward various aspects of crime and criminal sanctioning. The order in which an item appeared on the survey instrument was determined through random selection. Using an 8-point Likert scale ranging from 1 = very strongly disagree to 8 = very strongly agree, the respondents were asked, "Using the scale provided below, please state the extent to which you either agree or disagree with each statement."

As mentioned above, the questionnaire was developed with the intention of tapping the extent to which the legislators advocated conservative and/or liberal views on crime and justice. In constructing the items used to represent these divergent political orientations, we were guided by existing research that had specified how those on the left and right differ in their criminal justice views (Cullen and Gilbert, 1982; Gibbons and Garabedian, 1974; Greene et al., 1982; Miller, 1973; Shover, 1979). On a general level, however, it may be helpful to state briefly here our interpretation of the key ways in which the ideologies of the two political positions differ.[1]

The conservative position begins with the assumption that the primary goal of the criminal justice system is to protect the social order. They believe that a permissive society—one that lacks discipline—encourages illegality. When discipline breaks down in the legal system, people will soon learn that crime pays. Thus the way to reduce the intolerably high crime rate is to institute laws that make crime more costly. Of course, providing this lesson means handing out stiff sentences in uncomfortable prisons to offenders. The truly wicked who prove incorrigible must be incapacitated until old age robs them of their criminal propensities. Only in this way will the streets be safe to walk.

In contrast, the primary goal of the system for liberals is to see that offenders are treated with justice and care. Those on the left take this position because they believe that people come to violate the law because they are subjected to social injustice: poverty, racism, and neglect. The only way to eliminate crime is to attack these root causes. Meanwhile, those whose social circumstances compel them to move beyond the law should not be punished but rather rehabilitated and their problems treated. Imprisonment, a great deprivation, should be used parsimoniously, and when it is employed, efforts should be made to have conditions as humane as possible. Finally, everyone who comes before the court should be treated equally. Unlike the present situation, the rich and powerful—who often commit the most serious offenses, white-collar crimes—should not escape criminal sanction.

With these considerations in mind, an explanation is possible of how the items on the survey were grouped to assess various ideological dimensions. In all, four broad areas were distinguished: crime causation, views of crime control, support for imprisonment, and faith in rehabilitation. Within each area, several issues were examined, and liberal versus conservative views represented. Items were also employed that tapped a radical position on the issues. However, because none received more than a minimal degree of support (1 to 4 percent), these were deleted from the analysis. Briefly, the issues considered in the data are as follows:

Crime Causation

The basic comparison here was between the conservative view that crime is due to a breakdown of discipline and the free will of offenders versus the liberal view that crime is a reflection of root causes and an individual's exposure to social disadvantage. The items assessing these issues are presented in Table 3.1.

Views of Crime Control

This rubric encompasses four issues that relate to crime control and the operation of the criminal justice system. The first involves whether the solution to crime is in reestablishing traditional values, as the right claims, or in eliminating social injustice, as the left asserts. Second, attitudes toward the conservatives' crime control model and toward the liberals' due process model were inspected (see Packer, 1968). Third, items tapped whether the legislators believed that America's courts discriminate as liberal critics have suggested or, as those on the right would be likely to argue, that minorities are disproportionately represented among the prison population because they are more crime-prone. Fourth, attitudes toward victims were considered. The items relevant to the above concerns are reported in Table 3.2.

Support for Imprisonment

Here, three controversies were entertained: support for punitive philosophies of imprisonment (conservative position), opposition to imprisonment (liberal position), and whether efforts should be made to make prisons more humane (liberal) or keep them painful so that offenders will learn that crime does not pay (conservative). Relevant items are contained in Table 3.3.

Faith in Rehabilitation

Finally, a number of items were included that measured the extent to which the legislators supported the traditional liberal philosophy of rehabilitation. Did they see it as effective and worth expanding, or were they prepared to cast it aside and embrace a purely punitive approach to sanctioning as many on the right would prefer? The legislative responses to these questions are set forth in Table 3.4.

Finally, within each of the tables, we report both the mean score for each item listed (again, an 8-point scale was used, with 8 being the

TABLE 3.1

Percentage Agreeing with and Mean of Items on Crime Causation

	% Agreeing	Mean
Conservatives		
Breakdown of Discipline:		
1. A main reason why we have so much crime these days is because young people are just not taught to respect authority.	63.6	4.99
2. Crime has increased in recent times because society has become too permissive.	80.4	5.41
3. A main reason why people become criminals is that they have been raised in homes where there is a lack of parental discipline and where they are not exposed to adequate religious and moral training.	70.5	5.06
Classical Theory:		
4. Most criminals know fully what they are doing when they break the law.	96.0	6.56
5. Most criminals commit crimes because they know that they can get away with it.	66.7	4.98
6. Most of the people who violate the law do so because they know that crime pays in America these days.	48.0	4.42
Liberals		
Root Causes:		
7. A major reason why we have so much crime is because America still has too much poverty, racism, and social injustice.	46.0	4.23
8. Crime is largely a product of such ills as unemployment, poor education, and a lack of equal opportunity.	55.2	4.44
Positivist Theory:		
9. Many people commit crimes because they have very stressful emotional problems that they just can't handle.	50.5	4.40
10. Many people are driven into crime by the frustration they feel when they fail repeatedly at school or can't get a job no matter how hard they try.	55.0	4.70
11. People often break the law because they live in neighborhoods where most of their friends are getting into trouble.	57.9	4.57

high or agree side) and the percentage of the sample that agreed with a given item. Percentage of agreement was computed by adding together all responses that were greater than or equal to 5, where 5 = not sure but probably agree, 6 = agree, 7 = strongly agree, and 8 = very strongly agree.

TABLE 3.2

Percentage Agreeing with and Mean of Items on Views of Crime Control

	% Agreeing	Mean
A. Broad Social Control Policies		
1. Conservative: The best way to reduce crime in America is to re-establish the traditional values that made our country great: hard work, religion, respect for authority, and firm discipline in both the home and school.	84.5	5.96
2. Liberal: The best way to reduce crime in America is to expand social programs that will give disadvantaged people better education, job training, and equal employment opportunities.	69.5	5.11
B. Models of Criminal Justice		
Crime Control:		
3. The current crime situation suggests that we need large increases in the number of police and large increases in the number of prison facilities.	64.0	4.96
4. Because crime now poses such a grave danger to the tranquility of our communities, it is imperative that we hire a lot more police and give them the power to catch criminals, and that we build a lot more prisons to house these dangerous offenders.	49.9	4.48
5. It is an illusion to believe that simply hiring more police or building more prisons will reduce the crime problem. Unless we do something about the root causes of crime such as poverty and unemployment, the crime rate will remain high.	76.0	5.62
Due Process:		
6. While giving offenders legal rights may inconvenience police and allow some guilty people to get off free, these rights are important because they prevent the government from abusing its power and because they protect the freedoms that Americans cherish.	88.4	6.06
7. Criminals these days have too many legal rights because all the different court rulings often prevent the police from doing an effective job and allow a lot of guilty offenders to get off without any punishment.	66.3	5.13

TABLE 3.2 Continued

	% Agreeing	Mean
C. Fairness in Sentencing		

Conservatives—Courts Are Just:

8. The reason why our prisons are filled with poor people and members of minority groups is because it is these people that commit most of the crimes in our society. — 69.0 — 5.12

9. Whether a person is rich or poor, black or white, he will be treated equally by our courts. — 45.0 — 4.37

Liberals—Courts Discriminate:

10. The reason why white-collar criminals are not sent to jail is because they have the money and power needed to avoid getting caught, avoid getting prosecuted, and to avoid getting a harsh sentence. — 46.5 — 4.30

11. "The rich get richer and the poor get prison" is a fair way to characterize the way our criminal "justice" system works. — 24.8 — 3.38

D. Concern for Victims

Conservatives—Punish the Criminals:

12. If we really cared about crime victims, we would make sure that criminals were caught and given harsh punishments. — 67.0 — 5.17

13. We should stop viewing criminals as victims of society who deserve our help, and start paying more attention to the victims of these criminals. — 84.4 — 5.79

Liberals—Provide Services for Victims:

14. If we really cared about crime victims, we would make sure that the government would give these victims the financial compensation and social services (e.g., counseling for a rape victim) they need to get back on their feet. — 83.7 — 5.76

RESULTS

As seen in Table 3.1 (items 1 to 6), the legislators in the sample manifested considerable support for the conservative ideas that a permissive society spawns lawlessness and that illegality occurs when offenders make free-willed judgments that crime pays in America (this, of course, is the thesis of the classical school of criminology). Significantly, however, they do not see crime to be exclusively a by-product of the attenuation of discipline in society or

TABLE 3.3

Percentage Agreeing with and Mean of Items on Support of Imprisonment

	% Agreeing	Mean
A. Conservatives—Support for Punitive Goals		
1. Retribution: People who commit serious crimes deserve to be put away for a long time.	92.0	6.08
2. Specific Deterrence: Stiffer jail sentences are needed to show criminals that crime doesn't pay and thus to make sure that they don't go into crime again.	71.7	5.28
3. General Deterrence: Punishing criminals more harshly would reduce crime by setting an example and showing others in society that crime does not pay.	73.4	5.06
4. Incapacitation: Even if prisons can't deter or rehabilitate, long prison sentences are needed so that we can keep habitual and dangerous offenders off our streets.	91.8	6.05
B. Liberals—Opposition to Imprisonment		
5. Sending criminals to prison for long stays doesn't make much sense since it will only increase crime because prisons are schools of crime.	18.8	3.49
6. Prison sentences should be kept as short as is possible because depriving someone of their freedom is a very serious punishment in a society like ours.	10.8	3.00
7. Expanding community corrections is a more reasonable approach to the crime problem than simply putting more and more people in our crowded prisons.	81.6	5.44
C. Nature of Prison Conditions		
Conservatives—Prisons Should Be Painful		
8. While no one favors cruel and unusual punishment, prisons should be painful places to live in. After all, that's part of the price a criminal pays for committing a crime.	37.1	4.05
9. We shouldn't worry too much about the rights of prison inmates; after all, they didn't worry about the rights of the innocent citizens they victimized.	32.6	3.93
Liberals—Make Prisons Humane		
10. The main reason for putting offenders in prison is to deprive them of their liberty and not to force them to live in a degrading and dangerous environment.	69.8	5.05
11. Most prisons are in horrible shape and the only humane thing to do is to take steps to improve living conditions for inmates.	52.1	4.65
12. Inmates should be given all the rights that regular citizens have, except those that would endanger prison safety and order.	24.5	3.44

TABLE 3.4
Percentage Agreeing with and Mean of Items on Faith in Rehabilitation

	% Agreeing	Mean
A. General Support		
1. Rehabilitating a criminal is just as important as making a criminal pay for his or her crime.	72.0	5.42
2. I would support expanding the rehabilitation programs with criminals that are now being undertaken in our prisons.	84.8	5.56
3. Because inmates are good at tricking parole boards into thinking they are cured, all rehabilitation programs have done in the past is to allow criminals who deserve to be punished to get off easily (conservative critique).	17.9	3.58
B. Effectiveness of Rehabilitation: Does It Work?		
4. The rehabilitation of adult criminals just does not work.	41.4	4.24
5. The rehabilitation of juveniles just does not work.	12.0	3.11
C. Views of State Enforced Therapy		
6. Society has a right to try to rehabilitate criminals even if they don't want to be.	68.7	5.12
7. Inmates who participate in treatment programs and who show signs of being rehabilitated should be released earlier from prison than inmates who refuse to try to better themselves.	87.8	5.54
8. Participation in prison rehabilitation programs should be totally voluntary. Only those who want to be helped should be in the programs, and whether or not an inmate is involved in a program should have no influence on when he or she is released from prison.	29.3	3.88
9. Rehabilitation and the indeterminate sentence are just tools that are used by prison officials to punish politically active inmates; those inmates who protest the inhumanity of prisons or the brutality of guards are just kept in longer because they supposedly are not rehabilitated.	11.7	3.11

the courts. Approximately half also agreed that criminality has "root causes" in social injustices like poverty and denial of equal opportunity. Similarly, a majority endorsed the perspective of the positivist school (see Radzinowicz, 1966) that individuals who break the law do so because they are confronted with such criminogenic forces as emotional problems, status frustration, and deviant peers (items 7 to 11).

This duality in the legislators' attitudes toward the origins of crime—one in which legitimacy is extended to both conservative and liberal ideas—was evident again when their views of crime control were examined (see Table 3.2). First, although over 80 percent of the legislators agreed that reestablishing traditional values was the panacea to crime, nearly 70 percent also stated that the best way to cure the crime problem was to expand social programs. Second, support was found for the "crime control model" illuminated by Packer (1968). The legislators agreed both that there is a need to hire more police and build more prisons and that legal rights often reduce the effectiveness of law enforcement operations (items 3, 4, 7). But again, 76 percent felt that regardless of the resources allocated to criminal justice, crime will persist if root causes are not dealt with (item 5), and few in the sample were prepared to cast aside "due process" simply to enforce order (item 6). Third, almost 70 percent of the legislators concurred with the conservative position that prisons are full of minorities because this population is the most criminogenic (item 8), and 75 percent rejected Reiman's (1979) leftist notion that "the rich get richer and the poor get prison" (item 11). Nonetheless, about half of the politicians also recognized that justice was not equal before America's courts, a constant liberal critique (items 9, 10). Fourth, conservatives often link concern with victims with the punishment of offenders. For instance, in a speech favoring mandatory sentences, President Gerald Ford (1975) remarked, "The victims are my primary concern." In this regard, the Illinois legislators clearly shared this thinking (see items 12, 13). At the same time, however, fully 80 percent supported—perhaps because Illinois has a victim's compensation act—the more liberal notion (Cullen and Gilbert, 1982: 284) that the state has an obligation to provide direct services to the casualties of the system (item 14).

Table 3.3 shows once more that conservative thinking about crime had considerable appeal to the legislators in the sample. Here, there is strong support for all punitive goals of imprisonment and a firm rejection of the liberal notions that prisons are schools of crime and that incarceration should be employed sparingly (items 1 to 6). Yet this belief in the appropriateness and efficacy of imprisonment does not mean that the legislators were hard line in every respect. Thus they strongly (81.6 percent) endorsed community corrections, believed that prison conditions should be decent rather than degrading, and rejected the idea that inmate rights are of little importance (items

7 to 11). Although they stopped short of advocating a drastic expansion of inmate rights (item 12) as some liberal writers have urged (see Fogel, 1979), their views of what the nature of prison life should entail were clearly more reformist than punitive.

These progressive sentiments become even more apparent when considering the legislators' attitudes toward rehabilitation. First, items 1, 2, and 3 in Table 3.4 reveal that the sample believed that rehabilitation is "just as important" as punishment as a goal of sanctioning, would support expanding treatment programs, and rejected the conservative idea that rehabilitation is little more than a "con" that inmates use to win early release. Second, the politicians who responded to the survey also rejected the conclusion popularized by Martinson (1974) that rehabilitation "doesn't work" (items 4, 5). This was particularly true in the case of juveniles, where only 12 percent agreed that treatment "just does not work" (see Cullen, Golden, and Cullen, 1983). Finally, the legislators even embraced the traditional liberal policy of state enforced therapy (Barnes, 1972; Menninger, 1968; see Kittrie, 1973). As indicated by items 6 to 9, they did not see such programs as overly coercive, and they were prepared to tie early release from prison to an inmate's cure. This latter finding is somewhat surprising, given that Illinois is a state that passed determinate sentencing legislation during the latter part of the 1970s (Cullen, Gilbert, and Cullen, 1983).

CONCLUSION

In contrast to the popular stereotype of politicians as unenlightened about justice policy and as advocating a narrow law and order posture, the findings suggest that the Illinois legislators sampled were quite diverse in their criminal justice ideology. To be sure, they manifested a pronounced conservative strain in their thinking, trumpeting the importance of crime control and advocating stiff prison terms aimed at effecting deterrence, incapacitation, and retribution. Yet they also evidenced an affinity for elements of the traditional liberal agenda. Thus they tended to agree that crime has causes rooted in social inequality, that offenders have problems that are conducive to violating the law, that rehabilitation is an important goal of legal sanctions, that prisons should be reasonably humane, and that community corrections is an idea worth exploring.

Notably, these results suggest an interesting puzzle. Although the legislators' ideology was found to be diverse, Illinois has experienced a period since the mid-1970s in which the expressed goal of the state's justice policy has been to "get tough" with crime (Bigman, 1979; Cullen, Gilbert, and Cullen, 1983; Kolman, 1980; Lagoy and Kramer, 1980). Although initially conceived of as a way of introducing the "justice model" into the state's correctional system (Fogel, 1979), the determinate sentencing law that became effective in 1978 was explicitly coopted into a measure aimed at crime control. Indeed, the governor insisted on calling the renovated code "Class X crimes" to emphasize the law and order quality of the new statutes. Furthermore, since the inception of the legislation, prison populations in the state have continued to spiral upward. If the "Class X" code is not fully responsible for this trend, it has clearly been a contributing factor (Wingert and Zielenziger, 1981).

These observations thus lead to the question of why Illinois has become a "law and order" state despite the existence of an ideology marked by a progressive side within the legislature. Phrased differently, it raises the issue of the relationship of ideology to policy. Several factors may shed light on why the fit between these elements has been somewhat inconsistent in Illinois.

One possibility is that only progressive legislators returned the questionnaire, thus creating a false image of the ideology of the Illinois legislature. Although such a response bias cannot be completely ruled out, three considerations make this unlikely. First, the legislators in the sample, although liberal in some areas, nevertheless were quite prepared to endorse conservative policies to get tough with crime; they certainly showed no uniform inclination to be "easy" with offenders. Second, the profile of the average respondent was not that of a typical liberal. As mentioned above, over 80 percent defined themselves as either middle of the road or conservative. Third, it is significant that the results of the survey are fairly consistent with previous research. In their study of correctional elites (including politicians), Berk and Rossi (1977) discovered that their respondents clearly favored rehabilitation and other correctional reforms. Noting that their study was conducted in 1973, Berk and Rossi (1977: 147) went on to predict (fairly accurately when compared with the present data) that:

> If our study were to be repeated in 1977, state political elites would find their prison systems falling far short of perfection; and they would endorse a future for their prison systems that emphasized rehabilitation

(but not as strongly) and a more differentiated system of treatment of offenders according to the crimes they had committed.

In this light, a more promising interpretation than response bias of the disjunction between ideology and policy would be that questionnaires such as the one used in this study tap the personal rather than the "official" views of legislators. That is, politicians may well hold a complex view of crime and control in private but be willing to voice only a narrow, get tough position in public forums where the political stakes are high. This analysis gains credence from the research of Riley and Rose (1980) who reported that legislators overestimate the punitiveness of the public (see also, Edna McConnell Clark Foundation, 1984: 10-11). Berk and Rossi (1977: 145) similarly captured this point when they concluded:

> Elite views of the future also contradict what they perceive to be the views of the general public. The state publics are seen as endorsing punitive and custodial functions for the correction system rejecting community-based corrections reforms, and endorsing a future for prisons that would emphasize imprisonment as punishment.

Seeing the electorate in this way is, of course, a "reality" that few legislators would dare to ignore casually. In turn, this places constraints on how liberal they would allow their public images on crime control to appear, regardless of their personal ideologies.

A third approach to understanding the link between ideology and policy would start with the realization that the fate of any reform agenda is primarily determined by a relatively small political elite composed of influential and interested parties (Berk and Rossi, 1977; Travis, 1982). As such, the ideology of the average legislator is far less important than the views embraced by criminal justice elites. In the state of Illinois, the crucial actor was the governor who constantly trumpeted the determinate sentencing law as a way of cracking down on crime and forcefully pushed his "Class X" bill through the legislature. His agenda, and not what most legislators thought, was thus the most critical circumstance in shaping crime policy in Illinois. Moreover, for the everyday politician, this legislation was consistent with important portions of their ideology (i.e., a belief in the efficacy of stiff sentences) and had the added advantage of voter appeal. Consequently, there was nothing to lose and something to gain from following the governor's lead and supporting a get tough crime control package.

However, it is equally instructive that voting for "determinate sentencing" did not necessarily also entail a rejection of more liberal views on corrections; political convenience rather than a new ideology was the contingency at hand. This is why the legislators could support a law that abolished parole-release and still, legitimately, say at a later date that they believed in rehabilitation and tying release to treatment progress.

Finally, the possibility exists that inconsistencies in legislative "thinking about crime" are to be expected and, in turn, that the most significant factors in shaping policies are the prevailing structural conditions that give salience to a particular ideological dimension. This view begins by suggesting that such attitudinal complexity reflects both the contradictions that are inherent in general political ideologies and the reality that crime is an intricate phenomenon that defies easy explanation or solution (Finckenauer, 1982). Confusion in this realm has perhaps been heightened in recent times by the disputes raging among criminal justice scholars who, much like legislators, display little consensus in their pronouncements to the public; indeed, academicians commonly commence discussions of policy by speaking of the ideological "crisis" besetting their field (Cullen and Gilbert, 1982; Sherman and Hawkins, 1981). Thus given that complex, if not contradictory, beliefs about crime and control are to be anticipated, the key to understanding policymaking may lie in exploring how the existing social context determines which particular views will be seen as most compelling and have the most impact on voting decisions. Notably, this is the thesis of radical and other commentators who assert that political support for the current get tough movement is best understood as an outgrowth of underlying economic contradictions and the legitimacy crisis confronting the state, which make such hard line policies seem plausible and urgently needed (Cullen and Gilbert, 1982; Greenberg and Humphries, 1980; Paternoster and Bynum, 1982; Reiman and Headlee, 1981). In this light, the punitive tenor of Illinois' "reform" of its criminal code would be seen to be less a product of the conversion of all its legislators to a uniform ideological vision and more as a manifestation of a larger structural transformation that has conditioned policy in a similar way in states across the nation.

In sum, the nature of legislative crime ideology and its relationship to criminal justice policy is complex and escapes easy stereotyping or explanation. Nonetheless, the findings of this study do suggest some reason for optimism. Despite the unmistakable swing of American correctional policy in a repressive direction, there is reason to suspect that this has not been an ideologically coherent response to the perceived "crime problem." Although punitive sentiments have undoubtedly fueled this movement, it is less clear that politicians are wedded to an exclusively get tough view of crime control. To the extent that ideological diversity remains, progressive reform agendas—especially as the current crisis in corrections heightens and places pressures on legislators to develop fiscally feasible solutions—would be greeted with support. In particular, our analysis indicates that reforms might have the greatest chance of successful implementation if advocates (1) identified and then focused their efforts on political elites interested in criminal justice matters, (2) emphasized policies known to have ideological appeal among legislators (e.g., community corrections, rehabilitation), and (3) educated lawmakers to the reality that the public is less punitive and more favorable to liberal correctional policies than they now imagine (Riley and Rose, 1980; Cullen, Cullen, and Wozniak, 1983).

To be sure, some may question whether seeking to change how legislators think about crime is a fruitful strategy to pursue. Now, while we are sensitive to the position voiced most often by radicals (and alluded to above) that structural arrangements place constraints on what policies are possible (Platt, 1969; Reiman, 1979), we agree with Sherman and Hawkins (1981) that what politicians believe about crime and criminal justice makes an important difference in what policies will ultimately prevail. In their words, "It may be that the 'power of doctrine over reality,' which some determinists have dismissed as 'imaginary,' is not present or not easy to discern in many fields of human activity. But in the sphere of penal practice it is clearly manifest" (Sherman and Hawkins, 1981: 73; see Cullen, Gilbert, and Cullen, 1983). Seen in this light, within the broad limits imposed by sociopolitical relationships, efforts to "educate" lawmakers to the merits of progressive "doctrines" may hold the possibility, if not the promise, of achieving meaningful reforms (Cullen and Wozniak, 1982).

NOTES

1. In distinguishing liberal and conservative positions of criminal justice policy, no assumption is made that all political liberals will necessarily be "liberal" in this area, nor that all those on the political right will necessarily be conservative on crime-

related issues. Although we suspect that there would be a clear tendency for general political and criminal justice ideology to be consistent, it remains an empirical question as to the magnitude of this relationship and as to the social circumstances under which this consistency will be strengthened or mitigated (see Bynum et al., 1984). In this regard, the recent passage of "get tough" laws and the concomitant escalation of prison populations clearly could not have transpired if political liberals had not abandoned their traditional progressive vision in favor of an expressly punitive criminal justice philosophy (Cullen and Gilbert, 1982).

REFERENCES

BARNES, H. E. (1972) The Story of Punishment: A Record of Man's Inhumanity to Man. Montclair, NJ: Patterson-Smith.

BERK, R. A. and P. H. ROSSI (1977) Prison Reform and State Elites. Cambridge, MA: Ballinger.

BIGMAN, P. (1979) Discretion, Determinate Sentencing and the Illinois Prisoner Review Board: A Shotgun Wedding. Chicago: Chicago Law Enforcement Study Group.

BLUMSTEIN, A., J. COHEN, S. E. MARTIN, and M. H. TONRY (1983) Research on Sentencing: The Search for Reform. Washington, DC: National Academy Press.

BYNUM, T. S., J. R. GREENE, and F. T. CULLEN (1984) "The determinants of legislative crime control ideology." Presented at the 1984 meeting of the American Society of Criminology, Cincinnati.

CASPER, J. D., D. BRERETON, and D. NEAL (1982) The Implementation of the California Determinate Sentencing Law: Executive Summary. Washington, DC: National Institute of Justice.

CAVENDER, G. (1982) Parole: A Critical Analysis. Port Washington, NY: Kennikat Press.

CULLEN, F. T. and K. E. GILBERT (1982) Reaffirming Rehabilitation. Cincinnati: Anderson.

CULLEN, F. T. and J. F. WOZNIAK (1982) "Fighting the appeal of repression." Crime and Social Justice 18 (Winter): 23-33.

CULLEN, F. T., J. B. CULLEN, and J. F. WOZNIAK (1983) "Sanctioning ideology and the prospects for reform: Is rehabilitation really dead?" Presented at the annual meeting of the Illinois Sociological Society, Chicago.

CULLEN, F. T., K. E. GILBERT, and J. B. CULLEN (1983) "Implementing determinate sentencing in Illinois: Conscience and convenience." Criminal Justice Review 8 (Spring): 1-16.

CULLEN, F. T., K. M. GOLDEN, and J. B. CULLEN (1983) "Is child saving dead? Attitudes toward juvenile rehabilitation in Illinois." Journal of Criminal Justice 11, 1: 1-13.

DERSHOWITZ, A. M. (1976) "Background paper," pp. 67-130 in Twentieth Century Task Force on Criminal Sentencing, Fair and Certain Punishment. New York: McGraw-Hill.

DILLMAN, D. A. (1978) Mail and Telephone Surveys: The Total Design Method. New York: John Wiley and Sons.

Edna McConnell Clark Foundation (1984) Time to Build? The Realities of Prison Construction. New York: Edna McConnell Clark Foundation.

FINCKENAUER, J. O. (1982) Scared Straight! and the Panacea Phenomenon. Englewood Cliffs, NJ: Prentice-Hall.

FOGEL, D. (1979) "... We Are the Living Proof..."; The Justice Model for Corrections. Cincinnati: Anderson.

FORD, G. (1975) "To insure domestic tranquility: Mandatory sentences for convicted felons." Vital Speeches of the Day 41: 450-452.

GIBBONS, D. C. and P. GARABEDIAN (1974) "Conservative, liberal and radical criminology: Some current issues," pp. 51-65 in C. E. Reasons (ed.) The Criminologist: Crime and the Criminal. Pacific Palisades, CA: Goodyear.

GOODSTEIN, L. (1983) "Sentencing reform and the correctional system: A case study of the implementation of Minnesota's determinate sentencing law." Law and Policy Quarterly 5 (October): 478-501.

GREENBERG, D. F. and D. HUMPHRIES (1980) "The co-optation of fixed sentencing reform." Crime and Delinquency 26 (April): 206-225.

GREENE, J. R., T. S. BYNUM, and V. J. WEBB (1982) Crime Related Education: Faculty Roles, Values and Expectations. Chicago: Joint Commission on Criminology and Criminal Justice Education Standards.

HUSSEY, R. A. and S.P. LAGOY (1983) "The determinate sentence and its impact on parole." Criminal Law Bulletin 19 (March-April): 101-130.

JACOBS, J. B. (1983) New Perspectives on Prisons and Imprisonment. Ithaca: Cornell University Press.

KITTRIE, N. N. (1973) The Right To Be Different: Deviance and Enforced Therapy. Baltimore, MD: Penguin Books.

KOLMAN, J. (1980) "Crime and punishment in Illinois: The Class X question." Reader 9: 1:28-32.

LAGOY, S. P. (1981) "The politics of punishment and the future of sentencing reform: The Pennsylvania experience." Presented at the annual meeting of the American Society of Criminology, Washington,DC.

——— and J. H. KRAMER (1980) "The second generation of sentencing reform: A comparative assessment of recent sentencing legislation." Presented at the annual meeting of the American Society of Criminology, San Francisco.

MARTINSON, R. (1974) "What works?—Questions and answers about prison reform." Public Interest (Spring): 22-54.

MATTICK, H. W. (1976) "Reflections of a former prison warden," pp. 287-315 in J. F. Short, Jr. (ed.) Delinquency, Crime and Society. Chicago: University of Chicago Press.

MENNINGER, K. (1968) The Crime of Punishment. New York: Penguin Books.

MILLER, W. B. (1973) "Ideology and criminal justice policy: Some current issues." Journal of Criminal Law and Criminology 64: 141-154.

PACKER, H. L. (1968) The Limits of the Criminal Sanction. Stanford, CA: Stanford University Press.

PATERNOSTER, R. and T. BYNUM (1982) "The justice model as ideology: A critical look at the impetus for sentencing reform." Contemporary Crises 6: 7-24.

PLATT, A. M. (1969) The Child Savers: The Invention of Delinquency. Chicago: University of Chicago Press.

RADZINOWICZ, L. (1966) Ideology and Crime. New York: Columbia University Press.

REIMAN, J. H. (1979) The Rich Get Richer and the Poor Get Prison: Ideology, Class, and Criminal Justice. New York: John Wiley and Sons.

——— and S. HEADLEE (1981) "Marxism and criminal justice policy." Crime and Delinquency 27 (January): 24-47.

RILEY, P. J. and V. M. ROSE (1980) "Public and elite opinion concerning correctional reform: Implications for social policy." Journal of Criminal Justice 8, 6: 345-356.

ROTHMAN, D. J. (1980) Conscience and Convenience: The Asylum and Its Alternatives in Progressive America. Boston: Little, Brown.

SHERMAN, M. and G. HAWKINS (1981) Imprisonment in America: Choosing the Future. Chicago: University of Chicago Press.

SHOVER, N. (1979) A Sociology of American Corrections. Homewood, IL: Dorsey.

STEIGER, S. (1976) "Is expanded use of mandatory prison sentences a sound approach to reducing crime—pro." Congressional Digest 55: 220, 222.

TRAVIS, L. F. (1982) "The politics of sentencing reform," pp. 59-89 in M. L. Forst (ed.) Sentencing Reform: Experiments in Reducing Disparity. Beverly Hills, CA: Sage.

WINGERT, P. and M. ZIELENZIGER (1981) "State prisons jammed; Class X rules blamed." Chicago Sun-Times (July 19): 1, 4-5 in section 2.

ZIMRING, F. (1976) "Making the punishment fit the crime." Hastings Center Report 6 (December): 13-17.

4.

THE POLITICAL CONTEXT FOR THE CHANGING CONTENT OF CRIMINAL LAW

Anne M. Heinz
University of Chicago

Several recent studies have noted an increased invocation of governmental authority to address social problems through legislative lawmaking. Statutory content, whether in federal, state, or local criminal codes, defines the legitimate uses of state (i.e., public) power. The most frequent result of that statutory action has been to increase state involvement in the regulation of a wide variety of individual behaviors. See Berk et al. (1977) for a description of changes in the California penal code. It has also been invoked in economic life (Steinberg, 1982) with federal and state wage and hours legislation, and in social relations (Boli-Bennett and Meyer, 1981) with cross-national constitutional protections of children. However, the growth of governmental power is not an inevitable result of legislative action. Moves to decriminalize minor drug offenses and to restrict the power contained in judicial and administrative discretion in sentencing are recent examples of legislative action to reduce the scope of state power or discretion. This chapter proposes a context for interpreting

Author's Note: *This data collection was funded by Grant 78 NI-AX-0096 from the National Institute of Justice. Herbert Jacob and Robert L. Lineberry were the co-principal investigators. I was the project manager. The points of view and opinions stated in this chapter are mine and do not necessarily represent the official positions or policies of the U.S. Department of Justice.*

changes in the level of governmental attentiveness to one kind of social malaise—crime.

Numerous case studies of the lawmaking process have emphasized the importance of particular groups in the lobbying process. This study looks at the underlying structure of group participation in the development of law. In particular it looks at group participation in the local urban policy process as a precursor or precondition for systematic attention by state legislatures. One implication of such a view is that if the groups active in the local policy process change their level or patterns of participation, then the state legislative output will somehow be different.

The research builds on data collected by the Governmental Responses to Crime Project at Northwestern University. The original project was designed to describe the changing dimensions of crime and the ways in which governmental agencies responded in the United States from 1948 to 1978. Much of the work documented trends in 10 large American cities selected on the basis of variations in crime rates, demographic characteristics, region, and governmental expenditure patterns. The 10 cities are: Atlanta, Boston, Houston, Indianapolis, Minneapolis, Newark, Oakland, Philadelphia, Phoenix, and San Jose. The design is both longitudinal (31 years in the post World War II period) and comparative. It compares cities, states, and cities and states. (For descriptions of the overall project and findings, see Heinz, 1982; Jacob and Lineberry, 1982a, 1982b.)

The data for this chapter draw on content analysis of state statutory changes in selected sections of criminal codes; reconstructed histories of the ten cities, including systematic ratings by knowledgeables in each city of the content of the political agenda; and the importance of groups in the local policy decision-making. Finally, the work draws on a content analysis of an annual random sample of newspapers in each city.

The project conceptualizes two mechanisms for translating urban concerns into state legislative action. The first looks at the breadth and depth of group participation in the development of local policy. The second examines the information dissemination and agenda-setting role of urban newspapers. This chapter first discusses how the linkages may operate, drawing on available research. After laying out the design and data sources, it proceeds to test three basic hypotheses.

CONCEPTUAL ISSUES

Hypothesis 1: During periods of increased concern about crime, state legislatures make criminal law reform a major priority.

The variety of places in which the action may take place makes the study of criminal law writing interesting or difficult. "Action" is an appropriately vague term because I am of necessity addressing a complex mix. The quintessentially local or discrete event constitutes a criminal event or act. It is local in that it involves individual actors in a specific time and place. However, the forces that may account for that action are driven by historical developments that extend beyond city limits (Jacob, 1984). To complicate the scene further, the response to the accumulating crime problems may be made at a number of governmental levels (Schattschneider, 1964). Although crime may seem to epitomize urban blight, the definitions of crime and its punishments are made primarily by states although some federal involvement and varying degrees of local involvement are possible. Thus both the problem and the solution involve overlapping arenas of action.

The present task is to provide some substance to the term "historical developments," which affect both the problem and the solution. Although the immediate "causes" of criminal law revisions may be as diverse as responses to court decisions or publicity surrounding a particular crime incident, the aggregation of revisions will, I hypothesize, show continuity with patterns of urban political development. Legislative attentiveness would be expected to increase over time, as crime becomes a more important urban issue.

Hypothesis 2: Increased participation by a larger number of interest groups in local governmental policymaking provides an important precondition for increased state legislative attention to crime problems.

One of the characteristics of criminal law has been the reported domination by governmental actors of the law-writing process. Thus associations of district attorneys, judges, and police chiefs are some of the most frequently mentioned groups involved in code revision (Heinz et al., 1969; Roby, 1969; Berk et al., 1977; Fairchild, 1981). The importance of prosecution-oriented groups is probably not unrelated to the general tendency to criminalize behavior and increase penalty severity. At first blush, then, a study of the sources of criminal law would seem to revolve around the preferences of the law enforcement "establishment." The actions, preferences, or needs of other community interests would seem to be of little explanatory value.

Other research has suggested that the law-writing process is not necessarily a closed system. Heinz et al. (1969) suggested that if different kinds of groups, representing different kinds of interests were to become involved, the outcome might be different. Berk et al. (1977), on a related point, note that the successes of police groups and civil liberties groups suggest that the lawmaking process is not necessarily a zero-sum game: both types of groups have their measures of success. Quite a different picture emerges of the characteristics of group influence depending on the level of government, the law-writing stage involved, and the definition of law enforcement interests (Fairchild, 1981).

The perspective developed here is that the environment of group participation in which those agencies are located sets the conditions in which active participants take part. Furthermore, while relatively few groups may be taking a visible part in rewriting codes, the level of legislative support for those efforts will depend on the extent to which groups have been active even if on unrelated issues. Thus if unions or business groups incorporate support of criminal justice issues among their lists of priorities (or don't oppose them), an environment for action is created in which the criminal justice groups may operate.[1] They may provide legal and political expertise and legitimacy that has been filtered through the preferences of the established political interests.

Alternatively, with the organization of an increased variety of interests on the local level, the number and variety of interests addressing criminal justice matters may increase in the state arena as well, rather than being mediated through established law enforcement groups. For example, local chapters of the NAACP or ACLU, local bar associations, neighborhood groups, and civic reform groups now appear at state legislative committee hearings and speak out on sentencing reform, drug problems, and the like (McPherson, 1983; Buffum, 1983). Following from these formulations, changes in the pattern of relationships among the groups in the policy process in the urban scene are likely to produce changes in the state legislative responses (Hayes, 1981; Salisbury, 1969).

The density of group participation is one way to conceptualize the structure of group involvement in the policy process (see Beecher et al., 1981, for use of the concept in analysis of political agenda changes). Density refers conceptually to the variety of groups and their level of involvement as a three-dimensional space. That is, it includes information about the number of sectors of society that are organized and active in the public policy process, the intensity of that involvement, and the range of issues on which groups are active.

A group system is viewed as occupying space in the policy process. If the space is fully occupied, each of a wide variety of groups would be maximally active. At the other extreme, if the group space were empty, no interests, either public or private, would be involved in making policy at all. Over time and place, varying portions of the space would be occupied. Density may be compared over time and jurisdiction to see how differences in the patterns of group participation are related to the level of legislative activity. The density provides an estimation of an important external environment condition in which the legislators operate.

The concept of density may be used to describe an objective reality or a perceptual one. Measuring the two involves quite different tasks. However, the perceptual reality may play a strong role in determining the objective characteristics of participation as people act on their perceptions. Because the influence a group exercises is, in part, related to the importance attributed to it, the two factors are likely to be intertwined closely. In this chapter, I am closely interested in the perceptual dimension because it provides the meaning in the political arena shared by knowledgeable observers.[2]

The crime issue is one that does not have a well-organized "natural" constituency such as one would find in economic regulation. Action is likely to come when groups that exist for other reasons take up the crime issue. If the range of groups that are already active is small, the likelihood of success on the crime issue would be expected to be small as well (Hayes, 1981; Wilson, 1973). Because of the local nature of the perceived origins of crime problems and the tradition of local control, the source of initiations for policy solutions is likely to depend on the structure of the local policy scene.

Hypothesis 3: Urban newspaper coverage of crime serves an important agenda-setting function for state legislatures.

The role of newspapers in the legislative process illustrates the multiple patterns of group influence. Newspapers may shape perceptions of the magnitude of the problem by the amount of news coverage they provide. In this way news media help define the policy agenda. Berk et al. (1977) found a strong relationship between the changing crime rates and the amount of news coverage, pointing to the continuity between problem and agenda placement. Thus newspaper coverage serves as a source for policy action in the state legislature.

The local news media may also serve as important agents for the content of the interests of local organized groups. That is, group leadership in a city may develop their lobbying agenda from their perceptions of the content of urban problems as defined by urban news coverage. Thus news content becomes an information source for the entrepreneurial role of group leaders (Salisbury, 1969; Eyestone, 1978).

In summary, one implication of the view that crime is a local and peculiarly urban problem is that the pressure to act is likely to have its roots, not in the state House or legislative halls, but in the home districts. The crime issue is one that appears to rise or fall in part because of public concern and/or because of the political or bureaucratic benefits to be gained by the issue (Heinz et al., 1983).

DESIGN AND DATA SOURCES

The research used a time-based, comparative design, examining trends in ten cities located in nine states. The selection of the ten cities was made to maximize differences in social, economic, and political development. The work used a most-different-systems design (Przeworski and Teune, 1970). The task for the analysis was to identify those trends within cities that accounted for variations across the jurisdictions. Thus as much content as possible was provided to the terms "historical" and "cultural" differences. Each jurisdiction becomes a test of the hypotheses.

Before proceeding to the discussion of the different data sources, some general points about the larger project are in order. The data requirements for the larger project on which this chapter draws were massive, costly, and certainly difficult to obtain. The reconstruction of complete series of data for each of the jurisdictions raised conceptual and methodological problems, particularly in the recreation of perceptual dimensions such as policy agenda or group influence. In order to strengthen the subjective judgments of observers, I tried to triangulate among available sources. At each step, compromises necessarily were made among the competing interests of completeness, comparability, depth, and research costs.

Dependent Variable:
State Legislative Attentiveness to Crime

The work used statutory definitions of a variety of order maintenance offenses—disorderly conduct, drugs, and weapons possession—to examine the shifting boundaries of public authority to control individual conduct. To accomplish this, it traced the ways in which the label of criminal has moved, been enhanced, removed, or reinforced. The work examined offenses that are on the periphery where less agreement is found than at the core of shared norms for legitimate conduct. The behaviors are not insignificant social or law enforcement issues. They constitute a major portion of police work in most communities (see *Chicago Tribune,* 1984, for account of Chicago disorderly conduct case; Jacob, 1984; Bittner, 1974). They perhaps more directly address a community's perceptions about crime problems than does information about murder, robbery, or rape reported daily in the media (Lewis, 1982). Finally, because of the contextual base of their definitions, these offenses are useful measures of underlying social configurations.

This chapter used the sums of revisions adopted per legislative session (i.e., 2 years) in each jurisdiction to measure legislative attentiveness to crime. It did not incorporate any indication of the content of the change nor its subject. A revision was counted each time the definition or penalty of the selected offenses was changed. As a result, major code reform covering all offenses was weighted more heavily than discrete changes in a single offense. Over 400 revisions in the 6 offenses included in disorderly conduct, drugs, and weapons sale and possession were identified in the 9 state codes. The content analysis of the offenses was conducted by 2 coders using the *Annotated Statutes*. External and internal validity checks showed acceptable levels of data quality (Heinz, 1982).

Independent Variables

The work reported here used two independent variables, aside from a measure of time. The first was a summary measure of the concept of the perceived density of group participation in the local policy process. It was based on ratings made by knowledgeables in each city (Beecher et al. 1982). Typically the knowledgeables were local historians, city editors, and the like, as well as the local field director who developed an expertise across all periods. The ratings were made for each mayoral incumbency—a variable time span—that provided a useful anchor for judgments across time and location. Each incumbency was rated by an average of three knowledgeables. They were asked to rate how influential each of a set of ten types of groups (labor, minorities, political parties, mayor, municipal employees, neighborhood groups, civic or public interest [e.g., League of Women Voters], police chief, and the news media) were in encouraging or vetoing four kinds of urban policy issues: (1) economic development, (2) minority hiring, (3) intergovernmental aid (e.g., federal grants), and (4) budgetary policy. The informants used a 1 to 7 scale with 1 indicating that the group was of no importance at all and 7 meaning that the group was critical in determining the outcome. The average of all of the knowledgeables' ratings made for each group in each incumbency was then used for the subsequent analysis. To obtain a summary rating of the importance of groups that would be sensitive to a wide range of issues as well as their level of involvement, the sum of the ratings across all four issues and ten group sectors was used.

The summary ratings wherever possible were corroborated with historical sources. As evidence that increases in group density over time were not simply the result of better recollections of more recent events, the summary incumbency scores for three of the ten cities showed greater participation in earlier years than in later times, consistent with other historical reports.

The second independent variable estimated newspaper attentiveness to crime. The indicator consisted of the proportion of front page articles devoted to crime (Swank et al., 1982). The data were drawn from a content analysis of newspapers from 9 of the 10 cities for a random sample of dates. With these procedures, 6,500 newspapers were coded to produce annual measures of news coverage in 9 of the 10 cities. (Newark's newspapers were omitted because of the expected overlap with New York city news.)

File Construction

The data were organized into biennial series, matching the calendars of most state legislatures. The estimates of annual newspaper coverage of crime were summed and averaged to produce biennial estimates. Such a procedure served to reduce some of the annual variations that surrounded a trend of increased crime coverage over time. Biennial estimates of trends within incumbencies for group density were extrapolated from the incumbency based data.[3]

FINDINGS

Historical Trends

In 1948 Harry Truman was president, the Chicago Cubs did not win the World Series, only a modest portion of the households in the United States had a single television, and computers and jet planes existed only in primitive forms. In many respects the world was indeed different then. By most accounts the political world in 1948 was unbothered by the need to address crime problems.[4] For example, available measures of crime incidents showed relatively low rates— certainly when compared with the years to come. Newspapers devoted roughly one front page story in seven to crime. Furthermore, crime as a policy issue was generally not a high priority. According to knowledgeable observers, on a relatively uncrowded agenda for urban policymakers, crime took a back seat to a wide variety of economic issues (Jacob, 1984). In 1948 the range of groups positioned to influence urban public policy was relatively small. Based on estimates made by knowledgeables of the period, most interest group sectors (e.g., business, labor, community groups, police, political parties) played a minimal role in public policy decision making.[5]

From 1948 to 1950, the nine state legislatures together passed only a total of three revisions involving any of the six selected offenses. Thus, in 1948, crime was not perceived to be a matter of urgent policy concern. The urban policy mechanisms such as group involvement or media coverage were not geared to the issue.

As time passed, the relatively quiet urban agenda changed in response to the changing conditions and priorities. Riots, crime rates, poverty, racism, unemployment, corruption—by 1978, cities and the nation had become well aware of a number of these unsettling dimensions of contemporary life. State legislatures enacted more and more changes to their criminal codes.[6] By the 1977-1978 biennium, the 9 states, which had adopted a sum of 3 changes in the first sessions, passed 55 such changes, averaging more than 6 revisions per state. In most of the jurisdictions, the variety of groups perceived to be active in the local policy process and the importance of their contributions increased in major ways during the period. Civic groups, neighborhood groups, unions, business groups—their range, visibility, and perceived importance to the conduct of political life increased significantly in most cities. The methods of conducting urban policy changed, adapting to the increased legitimacy of the participation of numerous private and public interests.[7]

TABLE 4.1

Multiple Regression Results for the Density of Group Participation, Percentage of Newpaper Crime Stories, and Time as Predictors of Legislative Volume of Revisions

Jurisdiction	R	R^2	Beta Weights Group Density	% of Page = Crime	Time
San Jose	.85	.72 (.001)	.60	-.53	1.79
Oakland	.78	.61 (.002)	.70	.16	Drop
Phoenix	.75	.56 (.02)	-.67	.20	1.20
Indianapolis	.72	.52 (.03)	-.06	-.11	.77
Atlanta	.67	.45 (.02)	-.53	.30	Drop
Boston[1]	.65	.42 (.08)	.54	.11	.54
Minneapolis	.57	.32 (.18)	-.21	.04	.74
Houston	.44	.19 (.25)	-.08	.51	Drop
Philadelphia	.42	.18 (.10)	.42	Drop	Drop
Newark[2]	.37	.14 (.39)	-.25	N.A.	.53
All[3]	.56	.32 (.000)	.14	.20	.42

NOTE: Variable scoring: Higher values indicate greater group density, greater crime coverage, more recent time, and higher biennial volume of legislation.

1. Dummy measure of time used to indicate lull in legislative attentiveness to criminal sanctions and criminalization (1961-1969). A most likely interpretation was that the state was active but not in the punitive prohibitions that occupied its attention at earlier and later periods. This was a time when the state removed some of the status offenses, introduced zoning procedures rather than criminal sanctions to regulate pornographic businesses, and the like.

2. News coverage was not coded for Newark Press.

3. Test includes the nine cities for which complete data were available; Newark was omitted because of missing news coverage.

Testing the Model

Assessing the utility of an urban-based model involves evaluating the number of tests (i.e., jurisdictions) in which urban conditions explain state legislative attention. The initial evidence provided moderate support for such a focus. Table 4.1 shows the results of these tests. The R^2 values indicate the proportion of variance in state legislative revision rates explained by three variables: the density of group participation in the local policy process, the amount of newspaper coverage of crime, and time. The standardized betas indicate the relative strength of the contributions of each independent variable after controlling for the effects of the others in the test.

Over 30 percent of the variance in 7 of the 10 tests was explained by those 3 measures. When the jurisdictions were pooled, thereby grouping a wide variety of local historical experiences, the model explained over 30 percent of the variance.

Historical trends

An obvious explanation of the results is that the effects are artifacts of American history: What appear to be effects of local issues are, instead, tapping underlying national, not local, trends. Granting the caveats of small sample size (in each test sixteen biennial sessions were used) and measurement error in using historical reconstructions, the results are instructive. They indicate several points about the content of the historical trend toward increased legislative attentiveness to crime.

In fact, in four of the ten cities (Oakland, Atlanta, Houston, and Philadelphia), the time dimension did not add significantly to an understanding of the state enactment patterns over and above what the local variables contribute. In three more (San Jose, Indianapolis, and Boston), the historical trends were present but did not substantially affect the importance of the mobilization of urban interests as an explanatory variable in the conduct of state policy decisions. As an example, Figure 4.1 shows a near-perfect lock-step increase in both legislation and group activity, in this case for Oakland, where racial, crime, and economic problems received increasing local attention (Graeven and Schonborn, 1981). The model of local political developments captures some of the content of that residual term "history" for a number of jurisdictions that varied tremendously in regional, political, social, and economic conditions.

Structure of group participation

In 4 jurisdictions (Oakland, San Jose, Boston, and Philadelphia), the importance of local groups in explaining state politics produced relatively strong, positive relationships (see the positive betas, all above .40), as hypothesized.

In three others (Phoenix, Minneapolis, and Newark), what had been a positive relationship between characteristics of organized interests and state legislative activity turned to a negative one with the introduction of historical trends. Plots of the trends in state enactments and local group developments indicated that in each of the three cities, group participation, while increasing over time along with enactments, tended to precede state enactment increases. Minneapolis showed the process most clearly. Particularly in the

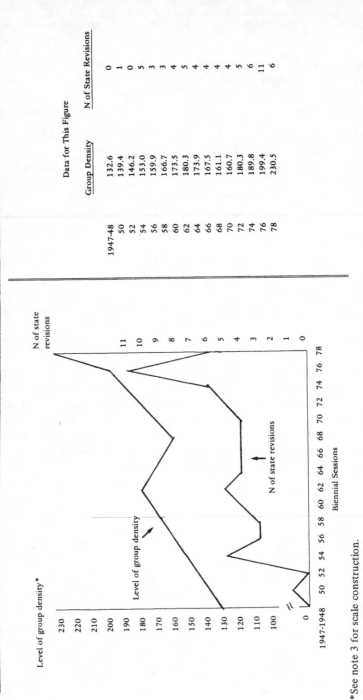

	Data for This Figure	
	Group Density	N of State Revisions
1947-48	132.6	0
50	139.4	1
52	146.2	0
54	153.0	5
56	159.9	3
58	166.7	3
60	173.5	4
62	180.3	5
64	173.9	4
66	167.5	4
68	161.1	4
70	160.7	5
72	180.3	6
74	189.8	6
76	199.4	11
78	230.5	6

*See note 3 for scale construction.

Figure 4.1. Changing Levels of Urban Group Density and State Legislative Activity: Oakland, CA

latter half of the period, increased group activity in the city was followed a session later by an increase in the number of revisions (see Figure 4.2). Minneapolis's history of weak mayors and strong community involvement created a situation in which organizational mobilization was an important component of political life. Consensus building among civic organizations, unions, downtown development groups, and, particularly in the later years, neighborhood and block clubs, was a prerequisite for subsequent policy action (McPherson, 1983). Thus for seven of the ten cities, the hypothesized model worked rather well.

For the remaining three, Houston, Atlanta, and Indianapolis, the explanation appears to lie in more complex patterns involving state level political conditions. Reapportionment and the weakening of one-party control and party realignments changed the state political scene. Based on preliminary work, with the changes in the political structures, even these jurisdictions became more involved in criminal law revisions in the later years. Thus a structural capacity to receive local input was undoubtedly a second precondition for state responses.[8]

Newspaper Attentiveness

The availability of organized groups provides a mechanism for articulating local concerns in a politically relevant manner. The content of news coverage of urban conditions is likely to be an important source for shaping the policy content of lobbying interests as well as urban-based politicians (Frohlich et al., 1971; Eyestone, 1978). In this fashion news coverage may directly affect legislative attentiveness by functioning as a major information source for state legislators. Finally, news organizations may act as interest groups in their own right (Berk et al., 1977).

The newspaper attentiveness to crime incidents was closely related to state legislative enactments. In Oakland, Phoenix, Atlanta, and Houston, the two increased together, even after taking account of historical trends. For example, the Pulliam Press in Phoenix, with articles about rising crime rates, was frequently the source of increased police efforts to reallocate manpower or increased mayoral budgetary priorities for police expenditures (Altheide and Hall, 1983). In San Jose, Indianapolis, and Boston, after controlling for time, the increasing press attention preceded legislative action. Thus in seven of the nine tests the relationship between urban conditions and state attention was supported. In the remaining two, Minneapolis and Philadelphia, the news

Data for This Figure

	Group Density	N of State Revisions
1947-48	133.8	0
50	133.8	1
52	133.8	0
54	133.8	4
56	133.8	3
58	133.8	3
60	128.7	2
62	123.5	0
64	142.2	6
66	160.8	0
68	179.5	3
70	168.8	5
72	146.0	6
74	158.5	3
76	197.5	3
78	181.0	5

*See note 3 for scale construction.

Figure 4.2. Changing Levels of Urban Group Density and State Legislative Activity: Minneapolis, MN

attention, which showed fewer historical trends contributed little to the state action.

In separate analyses that looked in more detail at the perceived influence of news media in the development of local policy, clearly the news media were perceived by local policymakers to play an important role as an organized interest. For example, in most of the cities a moderate to very strong relationship was found between the perceived importance of the media specifically and the general level of group involvement in the local policy process. The attribution of media influence appeared to operate in the same ways as that of other group interests. Newspaper editors and publishers thus appeared to join in the local policy process—to be a part of it.

The model of group capacity and newspaper attention as antecedents of state legislative activity worked with varying degrees of success in nine of the ten cities in the study. Indianapolis needs further attention. Although the overall model worked well there, explaining more than half of the variance, almost all of its power lay in the legislature's attentiveness to the historical trends in the state. The state's action seemed to be more attentive to general historical patterns, of which urban newspapers took part.[9]

SUMMARY AND CONCLUSIONS

The overall model of the structure of interest group participation in legislative attentiveness to crime was supported in a number of tests in ten different jurisdictions from 1948 to 1978. Although many questions remain in order to specify the process fully, considerable evidence supports the idea that the level of interest group involvement in the political arena plays an important part in stimulating action at the state level. Hence, the attention in a good body of literature to the processes in the halls of the state legislatures, emphasizing the traditional elite support for the growing power of government, may need to be changed. Apparently the actors who are most frequently named in the legislative histories may serve in part as couriers for a broader range of local interests.

Thus as the structure of interest group participation changed, so that more were active in the process, legislatures became more attentive to their concerns. As examples, a former corporation counsel in Boston indicated that his office kept close tabs on action in the state legislature powers, noting that Boston was generally successful in obtaining state action on city recommendations at least until the last years of the White mayoral administration. A member of the city council in that city pointed out that local groups went to their state representatives with their grievances rather than to a member of the council because the representatives were easier to get to know because they served smaller constituencies than did members of the council, who were elected at large (Heinz, 1982).

Local developments appeared to serve as the preconditions or stimuli for mobilization of the law enforcement community, tying law enforcement actors closely to the local political scene. Such a theme ran through the histories of these cities during the period. From police chief/mayors to politically derived crime waves, law enforcement has been an important element of urban politics.

A second point of interest involves the role of the press. Berk et al. (1977) proposed that the role of the press might be best understood as that of an established interest group in the political process—and that that role was different from its information dissemination role. The data presented here indicate that both roles are important in understanding the legislative process although the dynamics differ among the cities. Perhaps this provides some validation of the idea that crime legislation, which is often symbolic in nature, is likely to occur when the demands for action reported in the press come from newly formed groups whose voting strength may be unknown (Hayes, 1981). As newspapers turned their attention toward the coverage of crime, they have increased legislators' attention to the problem and produced revisions in criminal codes. Thus the role of the news media may lie in their agenda role that is translated into legislative action through the work of organized groups, of which they are one.

The findings presented here suggest that the states have been extending their reach through prohibitions and sanctions in conjunction with an expanded network of interest group influentials and a rising awareness of the problems of crime. Thus the state actions have not been unilateral. Rather, they have occurred in response to the changing structure of demands brought to the legislative arena.

NOTES

1. An extension of this notion is the idea that the density of group participation will explain the level of state action across a broad range of policy options.

2. I am indebted to Robert Salisbury for pointing out this dilemma.

3. In practice, this required making a decision about appropriate trend assumptions in the life of group participation during an incumbency. The same scores could have been repeated for each biennial period in the incumbency. The resulting stairstep line seemed unnecessarily crude in light of the developmental process likely to be involved. Instead, I made the assumption that the most salient or characteristic pattern would be associated with the end of the term. The difference in incumbency scores was then parcelled out equally among each of the intervening biennial periods. Thus, if the group density score for Rizzo's term (which lasted 6 years) was 125 while for his predecessor it was 100, the difference, 25, was divided into 4 segments so that an increment of 6.3 (25 divided by 4) was added to each period from the end of his predecessor's term to the end of his own. In this way, the slope of the line, which was linear within an incumbency, might change across incumbencies. Lacking any baseline information, the incumbency scores were used for each biennial period for the first incumbency. This technique may explain some discrepancies in jurisdictions with long first incumbencies—Atlanta and San Jose.

4. There were two exceptions. The first was Indianapolis where policy discussions about serious crime problems occurred in the late 1940s—juvenile loitering and speeding cars. This concern was reflected in knowledgeables' estimates that crime was a very significant issue in 1948 (Pepinsky and Parnell, 1981). The second was New Jersey where state officials mounted a major political assault on drug users, an issue about which local policymakers expressed little concern (Guyot, 1983).

5. The history in two of the cities, Atlanta and San Jose, each of which had dynamic and highly visible political leaders—Mayor Hartsfield in Atlanta and San Jose's city manager, Dutch Hamann—suggests that they consulted organized interests somewhat more frequently in the process of rapid economic development than did their counterparts in other cities of the period (Tucker, 1981; Betsalel, 1983).

6. The changes in these selected criminal provisions increased at a much faster rate than did the overall enactment rate in these legislatures. A rough estimate is that the legislatures were enacting approximately 1.5 times as many provisions in 1977-1978 as they did in 1949-1950. (*Book of the States*). The figures show an average 6-fold increase in the number of enactments to the selected criminal sections between 1949-1950 and 1977-1978. As a measure of the external validity of my data using a limited number of offenses from the criminal code, Berk et al. (1977) report a similarly greater increase in criminal code revision in California from 1955-1971 than for all revisions.

7. The list is long in many cities: the Committee of 70, the Pennsylvania Economy League, the Pennsylvania Prison Society, the Civil Rights Congress, and the local bar association in Philadelphia; the Pulliam Press in Phoenix; union endorsements, the New Jersey Conference of Christians and Jews, NAACP, CORE, and neighborhood social clubs in Newark; unions, the Downtown Council Civic League, bar association, and League of Women Voters in Minneapolis; the Community Alert Patrol, ACLU, bar association, and Police Officers Association in San Jose.

8. In Atlanta, the city council was extremely active revising their ordinances covering the same offenses. The substance of those changes often preceded similar state action (Vann Woodward, 1957; Heinz, 1982). In Indiana, the city-state relations were restructured in 1969 with the adoption of metropolitan government; beginning in the 1969 session the Indiana legislature adopted many more criminal code revisions.

9. Two studies have ranked Indiana's legislature as moderately innovative (Gray, 1973; Walker, 1969). Indiana was among the five states of the nine that adopted major sentencing and drug reform provisions in the 1970s. The state has acknowledged its

reliance on regional innovators like Minnesota and Illinois in its code revisions (Revised Statutes, 1977).

REFERENCES

ALTHEIDE, D. and J. S. HALL (1983) in Heinz et al. Crime in City Politics. New York: Longman.

BEECHER, J. A. and R. L. LINEBERRY (1982) "Attentiveness to crime in political arenas," in H. Jacob and R. L. Lineberry, Crime on Urban Agendas, Technical Report of the Governmental Responses to Crime project. Washington, DC: National Institute of Justice.

——— and M. J. RICH (1981) "Political power, the urban agenda, and crime policies." Social Science Quarterly, 62 (December): 630.

BERK, R. A., H. BRACKMAN, and S. L. LESSER (1977) A Measure of Justice: An Empirical Study of Changes in the California Penal Code. 1955-1971. New York: Academic.

BETSALEL, K. (1983) In Heinz et al. Crime in City Politics. New York: Longman.

BITTNER, E. (1974) "Florence Nightingale in pursuit of Willie Sutton: A theory of the police," in Herbert Jacob (ed.) The Potential for Reform of Criminal Justice. Beverly Hills, CA: Sage.

BOLI-BENNETT, J. and J. W. MEYER (1981) "The ideology of childhood and the state: Rules distinguishing children in national constitutions, 1870-1970." American Sociological Review, 43, 6: 797.

BRAITHWAITE, J. (1979) Inequality, Crime, and Public Policy. London: Routledge and Kegan Paul.

BUFFUM, P. (1983) In Heinz et al. Crime in City Politics. New York: Longman.

Chicago Tribune (1984) March 31: 1.

EYESTONE, R. (1978) From Social Issues to Public Policy. New York: John Wiley.

FAIRCHILD, E. S. (1981) "Interest groups in the criminal justice process." Journal of Criminal Justice, IX.

——— D. S. MANN, and S. M. TALARICO (forthcoming) "Sanction policy and southern politics: Sentencing reform in three states."

GRAEVEN, D. and K. SCHONBORN (1981) Oakland. Evanston, IL: Center for Urban Affairs and Policy Research.

GRAY, V. (1973) "Innovations in the states: A diffusion study." American Political Science Review 67, 4: 1174.

GUYOT, D. (1983) In Heinz et al. Crime in City Politics. New York: Longman.

HAYES, M. T. (1981) Lobbyists and Legislators: A Theory of Political Markets. New Brunswick, NJ: Rutgers University Press.

HEINZ, A. M. (1982) Legislative Responses to Crime: The Changing Content of Law. Technical Report of Governmental Responses to Crime Project. Washington, DC: National Institute of Justice.

——— H. JACOB, and R. L. LINEBERRY [eds.] (1983) Crime in City Politics. New York: Longman.

HEINZ, J. P., R. GETTLEMAN, and M. SEESKIN (1969) "Legislative politics and the criminal law." Northwestern Law Review 65: 277.

JACOB, H. (1984) The Frustration of Policy. Boston: Little, Brown.

——— (1982) "The rise of crime in American cities," in H. Jacob and R. Lineberry, Crime and Governmental Responses in American Cities. Technical Report of the Governmental Responses to Crime Project. Washington, DC: National Institute of Justice.

——— and R. L. LINEBERRY (1982a) Crime and Governmental Responses in American Cities. Technical Report of the Governmental Responses to Crime Project. Washington, DC: National Institute of Justice.

——— (1982b) Crime on Urban Agendas. Technical Report of the Governmental Responses to Crime Project. Washington, DC: National Institute of Justice.

LEWIS, D. [ed.] (1982) Reactions to Crime. Beverly Hills, CA: Sage.

McPHERSON, M. (1983) In Heinz et al. Crime in City Politics. New York: Longman.

PEPINSKY, H. and P. PARNELL (1981) Indianapolis. Evanston, IL: Center for Urban Affairs and Policy Research.

PRZEWORSKI, A. and H. TUENE (1970) The Logic of Comparative Social Inquiry. New York: Wiley Interscience.

ROBY, P. (1969) "Politics and criminal law: Revision of the New York state penal law on prostitutes." Social Problems 17: 83.

RICH, M. J., R. L. LINEBERRY, and H. JACOB (1982) "Police policies and urban crime," in Jacob and Lineberry, Crime and Governmental Responses in American Cities, Technical Report of the Governmental Responses to Crime Project. Washington, DC: National Institute of Justice.

SALISBURY, R. (1969) "An exchange theory of interest groups." Midwest Journal of Political Science, 8: 1.

SCHATTSCHNEIDER, E. E. (1960) The Semi-Sovereign People: Realist's View of Democracy in America. New York: Holt, Rinehart, and Winston.

STEINBERG, R. (1982) Wages and Hours: Labor and Reform in Twentieth Century America. New Brunswick, NJ: Rutgers University Press.

SWANK, D., H. JACOB, and J. MORAN (1982) "Newspaper attentiveness to crime," in H. Jacob and R. L. Lineberry (eds.) Crime on Urban Agenda. Washington, DC: National Institute of Justice.

WOODWARD, C. (1957) The Strange Career of Jim Crow. New York: Galaxy Books, Oxford Univerity Press.

WILSON, J. Q. (1973) Political Organizations. New York: Basic.

III.

*Politics and Accountability
in Criminal Justice Institutions*

5.

THE INTERACTION OF ORGANIZATION AND POLITICAL CONSTRAINTS ON COMMUNITY PRERELEASE PROGRAM DEVELOPMENT

David E. Duffee
State University of New York at Albany

Correctional practitioners have long acknowledged the problems facing inmates in the transition from prison to community. One set of responses to these problems is the formation of transitional centers to ease the transition to parole. Transitional centers, however, are not only attempted problem solutions (as elucidated in their goals). They are also public organizations or pieces of larger ones. A number of organizational and political actors may not always agree that those transition problems of inmates indicate a void in correctional system structure that must be filled with new resources and commitments.

Development of transitional centers is a threat to existing organizations and represents at least implicit criticism of the existing public organizations. If transitional problems are severe and frequent enough to justify a new organizational response, then, by implication, prison staff and programs have been ineffective in preparing inmates for release or parole programs and staff ineffective in accepting them. Even if a new program is seeded with "new money" and precautions are taken to assure the existing program that its resources are not being drained, those committed to existing programs are likely to cry loudly. New money allocated to transitional centers could just as well

Author's Note: *This chapter is a revised version of a paper presented at the 1984 Annual Meeting of the Academy of Criminal Justice Sciences, Chicago, Illinois.*

have been allocated to bolstering prison or parole programs and perhaps with the same results promised by the new program. The new program, then, threaten not only technological competence but resource flow. Finally, some transitional programs may threaten institutionalized positions (Warren et al., 1974), not only in the correctional process but in a number of established service networks. Parole officers, for example, find offenders in the community who are not yet on parole. Transitional center staff may compete with parole officers for available referrals, and center residents may compete with parolees for available jobs and community program slots. Those transitional programs that effectively shorten time served in prison may be perceived as treading on the judicial prerogative in setting minimum sentence. Similarly, these programs, by exercising prison release discretion, threaten the traditional domain of parole boards.

The potential threats to mission are not limited to other criminal justice actors. Warren and his colleagues (Warren et al., 1974; Rose, 1971) have vigorously documented the defensive posture taken by traditional community service organizations against newcomers. Although transitional centers may not threaten the institutionalized positions of these organizations as frequently as they threaten their own criminal justice cousins, the potential is there, particularly if the transitional centers and other community agencies differ over the perceived eligibility of clients or perhaps whether they are deserving. Those transitional programs operated by state agencies may attract professionals with liberal orientations on the one hand and may be removed from local political norms on the other. In these instances, transitional centers are potential threats to local service networks as well as to criminal justice networks (Ohlin et al., 1956; Black and Kase, 1963; Reid, 1964).

Any transitional program will need to meet and overcome in some degree the challenges that arise from these threats. Which challenges will be the strongest and which will be most debilitating if not met satisfactorily depend on the type of transitional program proposed and on the type of political field in which the program is initiated.[1] The actual program developed, in any case, may be explained by the cross products of differing organizational and political pressures and by the capacity of the transitional program organization to accommodate them.

This study examines adaptations made by one transitional program from its inception in 1968 through its institutionalization in 1978 as a regular part of the correctional process and an accepted member of numerous community service networks. The final shape of this program varied remarkably from its initial design. The central proposition of this study is that this process of accommodation among organizational and political forces is patterned and potentially predictable, although generally unanticipated by the actors who propose and implement such programs. Additionally, variations in the nature of transitional programs are better explained by reference to these political and organizational forces than by references to the correctional goals of such transitional programs.

THE CONTEXT OF COMMUNITY-PLACED TRANSITIONAL SERVICES

As stated above, the intensity and kinds of threats created by a developing transitional program, as well as the kinds of responses it might make, will vary depending on the nature of the interagency networks in which the new program will emerge. The context of this case history can be set with the aid of two figures that locate the emergent program within the correctional process (Figure 5.1) and within the continuum of local versus state resource and policy control (Figure 5.2).

Figure 5.1 compares the location in the criminal process of four transitional programs with fairly equivalent goals. The New York State Department of Correctional Services and the New York Division of Parole, by a memorandum of interagency agreement have established prerelease centers in each of the state's major prisons. Each prerelease center is a separate nonresidential unit in the prison staffed by a parole representative, a prison representative, and several inmate "resident counselors." Any inmate within three to four months of parole release may voluntarily attend the center daily and make use of its resources, which include New York State Department of Labor job listings, classes on preparing resumes and opening bank accounts, group sessions on dealing with loneliness and family adjustment, and seminars by community leaders on what to expect upon release. The Michigan Department of Corrections and the Pennsylvania Bureau of Corrections operate a number of prerelease centers that provide for residence in the community of parole release for somewhere between one half and three dozen inmates under supervision of a small (one- to six-member) staff. Prerelease center

Auspice:	Prison Authority			Parole Authority
Examples:	New York	Michigan	Pennsylvania	Minnesota
Residence:	Prison	Community		

Figure 5.1.   Types of Transitional Programs

residents actually reside in communities, visit families, or seek and take employment rather than write letters or "practice" for these experiences, as is the case in New York. Finally, at the other end of the continuum, is a transitional facility model used in Minnesota. These Minnesota centers are community residences, but their residents are legally on parole. The goals of the Minnesota houses are identical to the goals of those in Pennsylvania and Michigan: easing the transition to parole. The facilitating process, however, takes place on the other side of the parole door.

In addition, whether the proposed transitional program emerges before or after parole and prior to or after an inmate's transfer to a community setting results in important questions arising concerning the relationship of the sponsoring agency to local constituencies that can support or retard program development. A tentative framework for ordering a variety of these other factors that impinge on transitional facility development is provided in Figure 5.2. Figure 5.2 is based on Warren's (1978) and Spergel's (1976) proposition that communities are an admixture of two principal dimensions: (1) the degree to which local units have access to centralized power and resources and (2) the extent to which local units interact with each other. Specifying three particular points on these two dimensions, three basic political fields for transitional programs can be identified. On the left-hand side of Figure 5.2 are correctional organizations ("community run" programs) with minimal formalized attachments to state authority. Financing, policymaking, and legitimacy are primarily local processes. A classic example of a prerelease program

Community Run	Community Based	Community Placed
Bucks County (Pa.) Work Release	Minnesota Community Corrections Act	Pennsylvania Pre-release
	--------------------	Michigan Pre-release
	Massachusetts Department of Youth Services	

Formal Articulation of Vertical Linkage ▶

◀ Formal Articulation of Horizontal Linkage

Figure 5.2. Community Political Fields

of this type is the Bucks County, Pennsylvania, work release center established by Major John Case. On the right-hand side of Figure 5.2 are correctional organizations ("community placed" programs) with minimal formal attachments to other local units. Financing, policy-making, and legitimacy issue primarily from a central or state authority. The Michigan Community Treatment Centers are good examples of this type. In the middle of the figure is a mix ("community based" organization) with formalized attachments to both the local community and centralized authorities. The Massachusetts Department of Youth Services, as reorganized by Jerome Miller, provides one example (Ohlin et al., 1978), and the Minnesota Community Corrections Act provides another (Blackmore, 1978).

This case study will focus only on the right-hand side of Figure 5.2 (community-placed systems) and the middle of Figure 5.1 (residential prerelease centers). These community placed, residential, prerelease centers are perhaps the most common form of transitional program (DeJong, 1980), and relatively complete historical data are available on one of them, the Pennsylvania Community Service Centers.

A community-placed prerelease center program has certain structural characteristics that are crucial to program development. First, it is a program emerging from a central headquarters that operates the state prisons, if not parole as well.[2] This locus of authority assures a modicum of cooperation with the prison staff who initiate referrals to the centers. Such centers, then, are not likely to be starved for intake, a requisite for all developing programs. Prerelease, as a state agency commitment, also assures access to other state level executive and legislative officials. Relationships with centralized authority are built in and very helpful in terms of funding and attractiveness to experienced human service professionals. Community-placed programs can usually count on continuing financial support and, compared to other types of programs, on educated and experienced staff.

The position as part of a state agency, however, also heightens the political visibility of such centers. Community-placed prerelease is a statewide social policy concerning prison transition problems. Every center in the state is thus vulnerable to the mistakes made at any other center. All centers are open to the changing and emotionally charged symbolic meanings associated with criminal punishment. Therefore, the access to centralized power and economic resources is a double-edged sword. It pressures central office officials toward uniformity and standardization in prerelease practices so that they can appear credible and in control when asked what the prerelease program is doing. However, the means by which central office officials increase their certainty about program operations will create inevitable problems for the department officials running specific centers at the local level. Some center directors facing conservative local decision-makers will be forced toward practices that are more liberal than local or regional political coalitions usually tolerate. Other center directors facing liberal local decision-makers will be restrained from practices that in their areas are not only tolerated but accepted.

The state run, geographically dispersed system will be in constant tension between pressures for local and central control. Some degree of decentralization will always be present because central office administrators are cognizant of localized pressures and of the fact that central office policies will have varying and perhaps contradictory results across centers (McCleary, 1978). However, the question of which organizational dimensions can be centralized and which cannot will always be problematic. Moreover, previous decisions either to loosen up or tighten up may have long lasting effects on program substance, which in turn create new constraints on central office ability to command or let go and on local directors' abilities to respond.

DEVELOPMENT OF THE
PENNSYLVANIA COMMUNITY SERVICE SYSTEM[3]

Convicted felons in Pennsylvania are supervised by two separate bureaucracies, the Bureau of Correction (until recently) in the

Department of Justice, which operates the state prisons, and the Board of Probation and Parole, a division of the governor's office, which makes parole release decisions and administers parole supervision. Transitional programs were initiated under 1968 legislation that provided for "the establishment of prisoner prerelease centers and work release plans" (Pennsylvania Statutes §1051-1504). According to subsequent administrative regulations, the residential prerelease programs provided "community living facilities for those former residents of regional and state correctional institutions who no longer require intensive custody. . . . By participating in this type of a program the resident facilitates his own transition to parole and subsequent release" (37 Pa. Code §95.111). The prerelease centers were initially called "Community Treatment Centers," presumably following the example set by the Federal Bureau of Prisons, which established its first center in Pittsburgh eight years earlier (Glaser, 1964).

Plans for the initial center followed the federal model quite closely. These plans, as set forth in an interagency memorandum of agreement, called for joint administration of the centers by the bureau and the board. The bureau agreed to operate the physical plant and provide 24-hour supervision with staff called house managers. The board was to supply the counseling function by assigning one parole officer to each center. This officer would carry the center residents on his caseload. Importantly, the board, not the bureau, also had control of intake because all center residents were to be inmates who had already received parole dates. Center residence was originally designed to occur in the last 90 days of an inmate's prison term, which was roughly equivalent to the average period of time between pronouncement of parole acceptance and actual release to parole. Two centers opened under this interagency agreement, one in Harrisburg in 1969 and one in West Philadelphia in early 1970.

Informants in the bureau and the board differ about why this initial administrative agreement broke down, but they agree that it did not last long. Apparently, splitting the responsibilities for supervision of a residential program between two separate organizations was not an effective means to meet the diverse and immediate demands of the residents. Also, the bureau, if not the board, was seriously concerned with lack of speed in reaching capacity. The bureau saw half-empty houses as a threat to the viability of the new program. Bureau staff also asserted that decisions on intake to a residential program could not be made adequately by a detached parole board that is only concerned about a particular individual rather than about the social relationships in the center. Finally, actions taken shortly after, if not before, the breakdown attest to the bureau's commitment to expanding its community corrections functions, a province that until 1969 clearly belonged to the board.

At about the same time that the initial administrative design was breaking down, two significant events took place in Pennsylvania state politics. Significant amounts of federal dollars began to flow through the new state planning agency, the Governor's Justice Commission, and a new commissioner of the Bureau of Corrections, Alan Sielaff, was appointed. He was the first commissioner who was not previously groomed as a warden but instead had headed the Pennsylvania Council on Crime and Delinquency. Sielaff had a strong commitment to community corrections and the policy of rein-tegration championed by the National Council on Crime and Delinquency. Sielaff's immediate superior, the state attorney general, chaired the state planning commission.

Sielaff quickly converted the two prerelease centers into a new Community Treatment Services Division in the bureau and appointed a strong central office director, Larry Barker, to run the division. He quickly gained the reputation as the "Jerry Miller of Pennsylvania." Sielaff and Barker immediately expanded the new division with an LEAA grant. By 1972, seven centers were open and completely staffed with bureau employees. Barker organized the centers into six regions, each with a regional director who was responsible not only for center administration but also for the development of new centers and the creation of other community corrections programs in the state. Each center was staffed with a director and two counselors as well as house managers. By design, the Community Treatment Services Division did not accept staff transfers from prison but sought regional directors, center directors, and counselors with community service agency experience rather than prison experience.

This period from 1970-1973 saw, then, not only rapid expansion but a decided shift in ideology and public image. Barker traveled the state calling attention to what he saw as the cruelty of sentencing practices and openly challenging the power of judges. He painted the new mission of his division as one of emptying the prisons—a far cry from the initial interagency agreement for persons already approved for parole. In particular, Barker used the vagueness of the prerelease statute to make greater numbers of inmates eligible for center place-ment. By 1972, any inmate was eligible for consideration if he had served half of his minimum sentence, had served at least nine months in an institution, and had no major prison misconducts for six months. The centers were quickly filled, in a few cases with residents who had as much as five years to serve prior to expiration of minimum sentence.

This rapid and fairly unruly expansion had some internal negative consequences. Center staff reported that their programs could not successfully supervise the same resident for several years. They observed that positive staff-resident relations lasted somewhere between 6 and 18 months, but turned sour thereafter. Residents with long minimums still to serve began to see center rules and routine as unduly restrictive after this time period. Particularly if they were working full time and attempting to carry on a normal family life, long-term residents saw the return to the center each night as an unreasonable restriction. So, in fact, did most of the staff. Moreover, the centers had limited capacities (ranging from 12 to 36). Centers that had accepted many residents with long minimums were therefore stagnant, and other eligible prison inmates could not be served. Consequently a new program component called "out-residency" was added during this period. Out-residents were permitted to live elsewhere and report twice a week to the center.

Out-residency not only solved the staff-resident relations problem, but expanded the capacity of the Community Treatment Division enormously. This innovation probably gave greater validity to Barker's claim that the centers were an alternative to incarceration and certainly a greater validity to his threat that he could empty the prisons. He and his staff had at least a functional equivalent of parole, except that they did not wait for parole decisions.

Despite the evidence of backlash from some conservative judges and strong concerns voiced by the Board of Probation and Parole, this liberal expansion continued unabated through 1973. By this time the bureau had assumed the total operational costs for seven centers and opened seven new ones with a new 1973-1974 subgrant from the Governor's Justice Commission. By the end of 1973, many of the centers were carrying more clients in out-residency status than as residents. Each center had effectively doubled its capacity without adding a bed. The system had grown like Topsy, although some of the effects of this expansion were not fully realized until political changes took place in 1974.

Many of the most important characteristics of the current division program were born in this era, although these essential program features certainly did not resemble the original interagency agreement and probably were not designed by Barker and his staff either. Instead, they were consequences first of the expansion and second of its rapid halt in 1974. In other words, some of these features probably could not even have been recognized until well after they were in place. Perhaps most significant were the following: (1) Unlike many other transitional programs, the Pennsylvania centers gained virtual control over their own intake process, first by subverting the parole agreement and second by aggressively recruiting and selecting center candidates when prison counselors did not refer people quickly enough. (2) In the process of accepting persons with lengthy minimum sentences, the centers started a tradition of dealing with offenders with convictions for violent crimes. Programs in other states are often prohibited from accepting violent offenders either by law or through community resistance. (3) In these crucial formative years, the centers had extraordinary luck in avoiding fatal mistakes. Although some bureau and parole officials complained of unbridled discretion in the division, either such mistakes were not documented or actually rarely occurred. (4) Barker's charismatic, expansionist style left many specific program decisions in the hands of regional and center staff. The staff rapidly developed their own programs as suited to their own skills and to the particular characteristics of their respective communities. (5) The staff, though perhaps antiprison in orientation, also developed their own self-controls over expansionist excesses. Such a program could easily have gotten out of hand. However, alarmed by the negative climate produced by long-term residents, staff in their own discretion cut back on lengths of stay they were willing to accept. Moreover, because they regarded out-residency as a capstone in a gradual release process, they took the supervision of out-residents seriously. Last, although each center's approach to services and counseling varied, all center counseling strategies would have to be regarded as intense when compared to other prerelease programs. (6) Partly because of the rift with parole and partly due to the noncorrectional experience of the staff, the center programs, with perhaps one exception, did not play "the paper game." In other words, center staff did not see it as their task to prepare residents to "make parole." The orientation was almost universally one of preparing the resident for independent life in the community rather than one of preparing the resident's file to meet parole board criteria for release.

These elements were either solidified or completed by events occurring in late 1973. Commissioner Sielaff resigned to become commissioner in another state. Barker followed him. The governor was running for reelection, and his challenger was a strong one who was believed to be preparing to use the community treatment expansion and out-residency in particular as a political issue. Backlash from criminal justice officials, which thus far had been successfully circumscribed, suddenly threatened to become a statewide political issue.

The new commissioner, Stuart Werner, had been the deputy commissioner under Sielaff. He was appointed with orders to pull the correctional issues out of the gubernatorial campaign. This was done by placing an immediate moratorium on all new out-residency placements. This move was successful from a political standpoint but caused a certain degree of chaos in the program. Although the center staff had already started reducing acceptance of residents with very long minimums, a substantial number of residents had as much as two years to serve prior to parole eligibility. Moreover, all current residents in January 1974 fully expected to gain out-residency status within a matter of months. Individual, family, and program plans suddenly came to a screeching halt with a few of the most liberal centers looking at virtually no resident turnover for a year or more. Inmates in prison who had requested transfers to centers began to hear rumors that the program was shutting down. Although this was totally inaccurate, open center beds had suddenly become a scarce commodity.

This was the first of two major battles between the centers and the central office, but the moratorium on out-residency, which effectively was cancelled eight months later,[4] had rather unexpected effects. Rather than become a divisive force between residents and center staff, the out-residency ban, more often than not, united staff and residents against the central office. Center staff avoided the brunt of resident animosity by pointing to changes in regulations that were, accurately enough, out of their hands.

Simultaneously, many centers, particularly in the western part of the state, adopted a significant shift in individual intervention strategy away from individual counseling and toward systematic and frequent use of services available from community agencies.[5] Additional reasons existed for the shift from an internal service to an external service focus by the center staff.[6] However, it was functional, if not planned, that the centers began to stress a resident's reliance on outside services at the very time when they could no longer count on actually living outside the center.

The third significant "accident" in 1974 was the decision by the new commissioner not to replace Barker with another division director. Commissioner Werner, instead, elevated the six regional directors to the status of prison wardens and met with them directly.[7] The result was a decentralized program. Not only individual case decisions but most policy decisions (with the notable exception of out-residency) were made at regional and center levels. Because the regional officers were either close to or housed in specific centers, participation of center staff in management was high.[8] Compared to all other bureau units, the centers became grass-roots democracies.[9] Measures taken in 1974 indicated that not only did the centers display "healthier" social climates than either most prison units or community centers in other states,[10] but also in some centers virtually no gap occurred between the perception of climate reported by residents and that reported by staff.

These simultaneous trends toward staff-resident unification, management democratization, and decentralization virtually completed the Division of Community Treatement Services program. The outcome was appropriatley symbolized by a decision to change the name to the Division of Community Services. That these events, in effect, represented the final program outcome was "tested" two years later when the central office, influenced by another political change, attempted to "tighten up the ship."

In 1976 the governor decided to seek the Democratic presidential nomination. He ran under the slogan that government should run as efficiently as business, an attempt to capitalize on his own business acumen and the 1974-1975 recession.[11] Although his candidacy was short-lived, the immediate consequence for the bureau was yet another commissioner, previously the warden of the Allegheny County Jail. Commissioner Robinson's stated mission was one of efficiency and control.

Robinson's first appointment was a new division director for community services. The new director, Tom Baier, had previously headed the program unit in the Allegheny County Jail. Baier was ideologically Barker's opposite. Whereas Barker had almost purposively sought chaos as a precursor to change, Baier sought efficiency, standardization, and central office control. After a lengthy planning process, most of his plans were announced at the divisionwide meeting in March 1976. Policies covering 24 separate program areas were announced, and directives on most of them were issued shortly thereafter. Most significant in terms of their impact were consolidation of 6 regions to 3, controls on resident rent and savings accounts, additional furlough and out-residency controls, standardization of staffing patterns in the centers, controls on utilization of private halfway houses, and standardization of time-to-parole during the intake process.

The intentions of these and other policies were clear: elimination of perceived slack resources, concentration of decision-making at the central office, and uniformity across centers. Results were mixed. Anxiety in the centers was again rampant, as it was in 1974. The reaction to required staff control of resident finances was equivalent to the 1974 moratorium on out-residency and in many respects handled the same way: Staff unified against the central office. Resident anger, though intense, was generally directed upward rather than at center staff. For Commissioner Robinson, Baier was able to achieve (and in relatively short order) the appearance of control and efficiency. The division budget was indeed cut, and resident rent money began flowing into the state's general fund. In response to almost any particular question about "how centers were doing," Baier could respond with the appropriate memo, directive, or monthly report.

The strong central office direction had some positive effects for center programs. In particular, Baier was able to renegotiate an interagency memorandum with parole, closing off old wounds, and, using the power of the commissioner, he was able to negotiate other agreements essential to the new external service style of the centers. For instance, by dealing directly with the commissioner of public welfare, Baier obtained formal recognition of the center residents' eligibility for public assistance, a legal right the local county boards of assistance had long resisted. He also engineered peace officer powers for center directors and formal agreements with county sheriffs regarding detention of residents facing disciplinary charges. Both acts improved the capacity of center staff to institute greater due process in the center revocation process (see Duffee et al., 1977).

Some new policies had unexpected effects. For example, through 1975, centers had direct control of subcontracting arrangements with private halfway houses. These resources were used especially for inmates with alcohol or drug histories. These inmates were often transferred directly from prison to the private program, although they were carried on center caseloads as out-residents. Baier saw this situation as potentially hazardous as well as disorderly. A directive was issued requiring all residents to serve six weeks in a state center before transfer to a private program. Because center staff saw the first six weeks as the most critical for these inmates and also saw the centers as incompetent to handle serious drug abuse problems, they simply stopped accepting referrals with histories of drug problems. Although the apparent intention was both informal bureau licensure of the private programs and additional controls on out-residency, the effect was a reduction in the incidence of drug problems among center residents to 7 percent (compared to 30 to 50 percent in some other states).[12]

Many center and regional staff reported that their disagreements with Baier's actions were not so much substantive as procedural. They resented the unilateral approach, particularly after three years of autonomy. The impact, however, was probably minimal or even positive. Surveys in 1977 reported staff relationships improved rather than deteriorated, as once again they united against a central office threat. Power with some other local units such as sheriffs and welfare increased. Local center discretion concerning use of community service agencies, with the exception of group homes, was not altered. The unique styles of staff-resident interaction within centers remained unchanged.

Arguably, centralization did not occur. Although the average amount of discretion in policymaking, as reported by center directors and counselors, went down somewhat in 1977 compared to 1976, variability across centers actually increased. Reasons for this were related to differential responses across regions and within centers to the uniform strategy from above. By 1977, the interstaff relationships, staff-resident interactions, and center-to-human service system relationships of individual centers were so variegated that attempts to make all the centers more alike resulted instead in highlighting their differences.

Although continuation of the central office pressure for a longer period of time may have had different effects, that pressure was removed by Baier's abrupt resignation in the spring of 1977. He was replaced by the present division director, Charles Pagana, who took the position that most center problems were best handled at the center level. He operated by setting a general context for center activity but generally refused to prescribe particular actions. With some differences, the centers returned to their 1974-1975 mode of operation.

When yet another commissioner was appointed, he retained Pagana, praised the centers for their effective work (the first such pronouncement from the commissioner level), and formally recognized the Division of Community Services as a mature component of the bureau. In his words, "The centers would continue to do what they had demonstrated they could do well." The Division of Community Services had been institutionalized.

PROGRAM DEVELOPMENT AND PROGRAM SUCCESS

From the perspective of this analysis, the centers and the division as a whole had succeeded in weathering a number of political and administrative storms. They had done so by carving out an institutionalized position with officials in the prisons, with the Board of Probation and Parole, with the Department of Public Welfare, with sundry service networks each operating under different local political norms, and with their own central office, which from 1969 through 1977 regarded them as an experimental weapon, at times aimed at conservative judges and the more conservative parts of the same bureau, and at other times as a weapon turned against its own developers.

This achievement is in large measure attributable to the managerial and clinical skills of its staff, and in some measure to unanticipated consequences of purposive behavior, the peculiar ways in which unplanned (but not random) internal and external constraints combined, and random error (or luck). At the individual level in all phases of the program development, rational intent was evident, but few chosen objectives were reached. At the level of the division as a system, no guiding purpose was evident, but in general, there was a drift toward an outcome that appeared functional for the division and probably for the individuals it served as well.

The final organizational outcome bears little relationship to the ninety-day prerelease center concept that provided the initial agreement and little resemblance to transitional programs in other states. In comparison to many other transitional programs, the Pennsylvania centers are characterized by lengthy client stays, concentration on violent rather than property offenders, high use of external services, a large number of centers with relatively small capacities, high per diem costs, low program failure rates, low parole failure rates, extreme selectivity in the program intake process and high control over that process by the program staff, a small proportion of prison releasees served, low staff turnover, high staff education and professional orientation, and a noncorrectional and at times antiprison orientation among staff. In comparison to other community-placed systems, Pennsylvania shows a high degree of decentralization, or lower than expected central office control, and a higher degree of center interaction with other local organizations.

In this case, the community-placed prerelease program development cycle appears to have developed in the following way:

(1) In the initial stages of the prerelease program, central office concerns drove development because local ties had yet to be made, and centers were dependent on central support both for legitimacy and for intake.

(2) Political issues at the central level, however, cycled more slowly than at the local level. Central office officials relaxed control in periods between significant statewide events (such as gubernatorial elections) seeking to control the diversity of center problems through decentralization.

(3) Local officials used their greater room to maneuver to develop niches for their individual centers in local political and service networks. Diversity across centers increased tremendously, and the different characteristics of the local niches reduced the ability of center staff to respond to central directives.

(4) Significant shifts in policy at the central office level at later periods in program development required considerably more drastic administrative action than previously to get equivalent amounts of center response, and, in fact, central office policy change over time became more ceremonial than real.

(5) The transitional program, over time, reached a quasi-stationary position, or the program outcome.

(6) This outcome is more accurately described with reference to the constraints built into the program during its first cycle of central-local accommodations than with reference to program proposals or program goals. Whether this outcome was "successful," in correctional terms, was probably a matter of chance rather than a matter of design. But the program outcomes that appeared successful, in the correctional currency of the outcome period, were rationalized as intended. This program was then institutionalized but may not be replicable.

In other words, the appellation of "success" to this program development is a label applied post hoc when a complex sequence of solutions to multiple constraints was functional internally and externally and pronounced to be efficacious. Observers can, in fact, look back toward the proposed goal of "easing transition from prison to parole" and say that the goal had been achieved. They cannot, however, say that the goal guided achievement except in the rough and ready sense that the initiating goal was instrumental in mobilization of resources at a particular point in time. The particular linkage of ends and means that was pronounced efficacious was not built into the initial design but into that stage in the developmental process when the program became institutionalized.

Whether that outcome can ever be used as a blueprint for the establishment of another successful program is a proposition that must be seriously questioned. Data about a successful program may be used to gather sufficient sentiment and economic resources behind a similar goal to begin another resource mobilization effort, but the effectiveness of a program may be less a function of what it is proposed or designed to do than what it goes through as it develops. To assume that anyone could recreate the constraints that led to success strains credibility. This assumption is a rationalization of history and a poor guide to implementation.

If this version of community-placed program implementation is credible, a rationalistic version of program success and failure is not viable, and decisions to fund programs on the basis of initial program design are naive. However, the practical result should probably be greater activism in program planning and development rather than the reverse. An arguable conclusion of this dynamic view of program development is that almost any program starting point has a potential for success. The view that anything may work (and may, just as likely, fail) is better than taking the view that "nothing works." Exemplary projects may not be the best guides in selecting the next program, but program planners can learn as much from failures as successes because attention should be focused on how a program can turn constraints into opportunities rather than on claims about how to ease the transition to parole.

An example of a similar developmental process in community-placed transitional programming but with a different program outcome is the Michigan prerelease system. This system, initiated with the same goals, was shaped by different constraints. The program in Michigan also qualifies as a success in the sense that it has reached an institutionalized position. The Michigan prerelease program is the second largest in the country in terms of residential capacity and in terms of proportion of inmates served.[13] Michigan, unlike Pennsylvania, has a unified prison and parole administration. Consequently, Michigan has used a number of center staffing patterns unavailable in

Pennsylvania. Larger Michigan centers have their own full-time staff, but centers in smaller population centers have been staffed with parole officers.

Although developed during the same period as the Pennsylvania centers, Michigan centers have gone in a different direction. Whereas the Pennsylvania prerelease centers stress intense intervention with individual clients, Michigan centers stress their utility as a screening device for parole selection (Johnson and Kime, 1975). That is, the Michigan Department of Correction takes the position that clients who successfully conform to center program rules are good risks for parole, and those who fail in centers are poor risks. The center stay itself is not seen as an intervention process but as a screening device. High program failure rates are tolerated under the assumption that persons unfit for parole have thus been eliminated from consideration.[14]

Whereas Pennsylvania centers have succeeded as a program that prepares a small, select group of prisoners for parole, Michigan centers have succeeded as a program that tests whether a large number of prisoners are already prepared for parole. Both states began with the federal ninety-day prerelease model. Michigan retained it; Pennsylvania did not. Both programs succeeded in establishing domains, but with contrasting proficiencies. Ironically, the Michigan success, which processes large numbers of offenders into community settings, developed under the rubric of a conservative social defense ideology, whereas the Pennsylvania success, which processes a small number of offenders, developed under the rubric of a liberal, empty-the-prison ideology. The outcome in either case could not have been predicted from the starting points, but both successes are related to system capacities to adapt to changing constraints in their varying political fields. Although both systems are prerelease, residential centers, as depicted in Figure 5.1, their differences can be explained by shifts in the political fields depicted in Figure 5.2. Michigan remained a centralized, community-placed system. The majority of decisions regarding client flow and program services are still made at the central office, and the primary transition function remains the one of transferring center residents to parole supervision. In contrast, the Pennsylvania system, at a critical point in its development, relaxed central control and permitted center staff the discretion to elaborate their programs in ways that maximized responsiveness in local service markets. Later attempts to reassert control had effects but often not the intended ones. As a result Pennsylvania ended up with intensive, change-oriented centers rather than parole screening devices. The Pennsylvania centers, in other words, formalized their relationship with local service networks and shifted from a community-placed field to a community-based field. Although the goal of easing transition to parole initiated both programs, differing political and organizational constraints encountered during the developmental process have meant that success of the two programs was ultimately defined in very different terms.

NOTES

1. Which kind of transitional program even reaches proposal stage is also, to be sure, influenced by these same factors. One could hypothesize, for example, that both Michigan and Pennsylvania state correctional departments were in better strategic positions than, say, the New York department to propose residential prerelease centers. This could mean that they had greater power to resist localized opposition to such a program or could mean the departmental coalition (Zald and Berger, 1978) favoring such an innovation was stronger than the resistances in the department, relative to New York. Observation and anecdote would suggest both hypotheses are likely true. This issue is beyond the scope of this chapter, however, which focuses on changes in program development rather than factors that impede or facilitate a proposal.

2. Whether the prison and parole administration is unified (as is the case in Michigan) or bifurcated (as is the case in Pennsylvania) is extremely important because this variable determines whether domain conflict between prerelease and parole can be settled through appeal to higher authority or only through interagency negotiation. This point will be discussed briefly in the last section of this chapter.

3. This descriptive analysis is based on data collected between 1974 and 1982. The quantitative data summarized in the following footnotes were collected between 1974 and 1977 when I was the principal investigator in a series of evaluation contracts between the Pennsylvania Bureau of Corrections and the Pennsylvania Governor's Justice Commission. A series of seven technical reports was issued during the evaluation. These reports are available from the commission (now the Governor's Commission on Crime and Delinquency). Structured interviews were conducted with all staff in the bureau central office and in the centers in 1974, 1975, 1976, and 1977. Questionnaires were administered to residents and staff in 1974 and 1977. Since the termination of the contract, I have continued to maintain contact with both regional directors, center staff, and the division director. In addition to the quantitative data, extensive use has been made of program monthly reports, bureau directives, and policy statements and field notes based on hundreds of hours of observation and discussion with both central office and center staff. I express my admiration and gratitude to the entire bureau staff for their openness and willingness to have their problems as well as successes discussed and analyzed in print.

4. Officially, the moratorium on out-residency was lifted eight months later in August, 1974, but the "reinstatement" included so many restrictions on placement that most residents were ineligible for out-residency. The central office required new out-residents to have medical justifications for living outside the center or documentations of family and/or employment complications that were difficult to complete. Centers found some new methods of dealing with this cancellation but not until 1977. Bitterness and disappointment about the out-residency policy changes were still strong among center staff three years later.

5. One center went so far as to refer out not only vocational training, education, and employment problems, but also virtually all traditional counseling functions. Said this center director, "We've shifted from rehabilitation to reintegration. We don't want our residents becoming dependent on the center. If they need counseling, we'll help them get it from the local counseling center." This director shuddered at someone's suggestion that the center start a softball team. "The last thing we want," he said, "is for these men to find their friends and entertainment here—and I mean either staff or other residents. If they want to play softball, they should join teams at the Y."

6. Not to be underestimated is simple maturation of the centers. Interorganizational service arrangements are difficult to consummate. All centers improved their service referral linkages between 1974 and 1977, and a positive correlation was found between center age and strength of service linkage.

7. Reasons for these decisions are speculative. Perhaps a strong central office division director was a more visible target for the governor's challenger in the 1974 race. Barker certainly would have been one. With the charisma gone and no one in the director's chair, conservatives had to point at six regional directors, none of whom symbolized a statewide program. Another possibility is that during this time of trouble, the commissioner decided to control the regional directors himself rather than through a central office director. That is, the decision to leave the division leaderless at the division level may have been seen as a centralization move. If so, it had exactly the opposite effects.

8. A number of center and regional directors made conscious efforts to include not only counselors but at least full-time house managers in almost all decisions. One regional office allowed the secretary and student interns to vote on significant decisions and to participate in supervision of cases.

9. Democratization had many facets, not the least of which was an ad hoc job enrichment. Center directors were not adverse to manning the reception desk while house managers were out in the field developing job contacts.

10. Moos's (1975) Correctional Institutions Environment Scale was employed. The centers were less control- and order-oriented than Moos's community center norms and more practically oriented. Centers also showed high degrees of support and spontaneity.

11. He was a self-made millionaire who had built an electronics empire before becoming governor.

12. Comparative resident problem data are available in D. Duffee and D. Clark (forthcoming).

13. In Michigan, 40 percent of all paroles issued are granted to persons who previously resided in prerelease centers (Michigan Department of Corrections, 1978).

14. The department points out, and probably correctly, that program failures are often less costly than parole failures. A program failure can be triggered by violation of program rules rather than commission of new crimes and returned to prison quickly (under Meachum v. Fano 96 S. Ct. 2536, 1976). Revocation from parole requires higher evidentiary standards of wrongdoing. Wrongdoing by parolees is also less likely to be observed because parole contact is intermittent whereas staff-resident contact in centers occurs on a daily basis.

The data on the Michigan development were collected in 1977-1978. I relied heavily on interviews with the department director of research and evaluation, the director of the community treatment centers, and the principal trainer of center staff. In addition, heavy reliance was placed on official documents and evaluation reports by Community Corrections Resource Programs (1974). Obviously, these sources are not nearly so rich or varied as the data on the Pennsylvania developments, but the information regarding the significant differences in central office versus local center control and conservative versus liberal political regimes appears to be reliable.

REFERENCES

BLACK, B. J. and H. M. KASE (1963) "Interagency cooperation in rehabilitation and mental health." Social Service Review 37: 26-32.

BLACKMORE, J. (1978) "Minnesota's community corrections act takes hold." Corrections Magazine (March): 46-56.

Community Corrections Resource Programs (1974) State of Michigan Corrections Centers, Analysis and Recommendations. Ann Arbor, MI: Community Corrections Resource Programs.

DeJONG, W. (1980) American Prisons and Jails, Volume V: Supplemental Report—Adult Pre-Release Facilities. Washington DC: National Institute of Justice.

DUFFEE, D. and D. CLARK (forthcoming) "The frequency and classification of the needs of offenders in community settings." Journal of Criminal Justice.

DUFFEE, D., J. MAHER, and S. LAGOY (1977) "Administrative due process in community pre-parole programs." Criminal Law Bulletin 13: (September/October): 383-400.

GLASER, D. (1964) The Effectiveness of a Prison and Parole System. Indianapolis, IN: Bobbs-Merrill.

JOHNSON, P. and W. KIME (1975) "Performance screening—A new correctional synthesis." Lansing, MI: Michigan Department of Corrections (mimeograph).

McCLEARY, R. (1978) Dangerous Men: The Sociology of Parole. Beverly Hills, CA: Sage.

Michigan Department of Corrections (1978) Annual Report. Lansing, MI: Department of Corrections.

MOOS, R. (1975) The Evaluation of Correctional and Community Settings. New York: Wiley.

OHLIN, L., R. COATES, and A. MILLER (1978) Reforming Juvenile Correction: The Massachusetts Experience. Cambridge, MA: Ballinger.

OHLIN, L., H. PIVEN, and D. PAPPENFORT (1956) "Major dilemmas of the social worker in probation and parole." National Probation and Parole Association Journal, II (July): 211-225.

REID, W. (1964) "Interagency coordination in delinquency prevention and control." Social Service Review 28 (March): 418-428.

ROSE, S. (1971) Betrayal of the Poor. Cambridge, MA: Schenkman.

SPERGEL, I. (1976) "Interactions between community structure, delinquency and social policy in the inner city," in M. Klein, (ed.) The Juvenile Justice System. Beverly Hills, CA: Sage.

WARREN, R. (1978) Community in America, Third Edition. Chicago: Rand McNally.

——— S. ROSE, and A. BERGUNDER (1974) The Structure of Urban Reform. Lexington, MA: Lexington Books.

ZALD, M. and M. A. BERGER (1978) "Social movements in organizations: Coup d'etat, insurgency, and mass movements." American Journal of Sociology, 83 (January): 823-861.

6.

POLITICAL INTERFERENCE VERSUS POLITICAL ACCOUNTABILITY IN MUNICIPAL POLICING

Dorothy Guyot
Center for Policy Research

> Police policy is public policy. Virtually no matters of a policy nature do not impinge upon the public. The involvement of the client in policy formation is an important goal.

George O'Connor (1976) made this observation after having served in four departments, two of which he managed. This call for public policy voiced by increasing numbers of police managers is a break from the advocacy of freedom from political direction. Since the turn of the century, progressive police administrators have fought hardest to remove decisions on hiring, assignment, and promotion from the influence of powerful individuals outside the department and to end corrupt ties to political bosses. They were correct in their assessments that internal accountability was not possible in the face of pervasive political interference. In striving to insulate police departments from interference, however, they rebuffed all policy direction. Their protective wall was the fiction that policies were unnecessary

Author's Note: *The welcome given to social science inquiry by George W. O'Connor has made this study possible. My thinking on the issues of political direction for police departments has benefited greatly from the observations of Daniel P. Guido, an experienced police manager, and Robert A. Stierer, an experienced city manager. Mary Stierer's clipping file has provided many useful details. For collegial criticisms, I am indebted to Erika Fairchild, Fred Meyer, Samuel Walker, Mary Ann Wycoff, and Roger Parks.*

because police departments simply and automatically apply the law to lawbreakers. The traditions of secrecy in policing and a long-standing reluctance of many police chiefs to engage in public debate give reason to suppose that the prevailing low levels of political accountability are exclusively the fault of police leadership. Not so. This chapter examines a decade of political events in a city where the police manager sought to develop accountability based on informed debate on police issues but met little success.

When police policies are made by agencies or individuals outside of the police department, power is being exercised over the actions of police department members. Power is defined here as the ability to get someone to do something that he or she would not have done otherwise. As in daily speech, accountability is an appropriate and responsible exercise of power, and interference is irresponsible. This chapter attempts to develop a reasonable set of criteria, appropriate to late twentieth-century America, for distinguishing responsible from irresponsible exercises of power in directing municipal police.

Political accountability occurs when governmental agencies and officials outside the police department formulate policy and obtain adherence to policy. Direct accountability to citizens will be excluded from this discussion. For example, when a citizen asks for and obtains traffic enforcement against speeders on his or her block or phones a sergeant to obtain an apology from an officer for a rude remark, that is direct accountability. When a citizen channels the same demands through a city council member, that is political accountability. In contrast to both of these forms of accountability is internal accountability, by which supervisors and managers within the police department make and direct the implementation of policy. This discussion excludes internal accountability in order to concentrate attention on policies made outside the department. The chapter also omits consideration of personnel issues in order to concentrate on service issues.

DISTINCTIONS BETWEEN
POLITICAL ACCOUNTABILITY
AND INTERFERENCE

The setting of priorities among goals is an act of political accountability. City executives and legislatures are appropriate bodies to make the difficult choices of what problems to address, what levels of services to provide, and what mix of policies to pursue. In regard to specific policies, one may distinguish between accountability and interference by using a framework for performance measurement developed by the Indiana University Workshop in Political Theory and Policy Analysis (Whitaker et al., 1980). Police policies may be measured against five different types of criteria: legality, effectiveness, efficiency, equity, and fiscal integrity. A particular policy may meet the test of accountability on one criterion and fail the test on another.

Legality is the requirement that all members of a police department obey the law. For most government agencies this requirement falls particularly upon individuals in policymaking positions because they have most opportunity to break the law. Because in police work the greatest discretion is exercised by street-level officers, the requirement falls most heavily upon them. Violations of the law include actions that are feared and despised: shooting citizens for no good reason, beating of prisoners in custody, placing under surveillance citizens who have broken no law, and taking bribes. Any directives by city officials for police officers to take illegal actions are political interference. All policies that are legal meet this test of accountability, whether or not they are in other ways misguided.

Effectiveness criteria are the ones most frequently used to assess policies and performance. Effectiveness may be viewed as the ability of a policy to achieve a goal or to resolve a problem. A first distinction to be made in sorting out public debates over police effectiveness is whether the debate focuses on the nature and importance of the problem or on the techniques of the solution. This distinction between problems and solutions is far from clear because the very way in which a problem is formulated implies a solution. In general, when problems are the issue, the demand is phrased, "Somebody do something!" When the solution is at issue, the demand is, "Do it!" Depending upon the way a problem is identified, one or more organizations may be held responsible. If there is agreement that a particular organization is responsible for the problem, this is equivalent to saying that some goals exist for the organization's performance, however vague, and that the organization has not met those goals. That is, problems are specific instances of unmet goals. Sometimes, however, goals are muddled. Measurement of effectiveness requires that the goals be clear enough so that an observer can discern whether they have been met.

Every organization may be regarded as having goals in many different areas. Because an organization can be more or less effective in achieving the various goals, no single question of effectiveness exists but there are as many questions of effectiveness as there are goals (Whitaker et al., 1980; Hrebiniak, 1978). Moreover, its goals are defined by a variety of constituencies: management, staff, other organizations from which it receives inputs and to which it gives outputs, and consumers or clients. Any of the constituencies may hold up a goal against which to measure departmental performance, and these goals may be in conflict. Among the welter of goals, the ones that actually influence what members of the agency do in their organizational roles are operational policy.

When an organization is not effective in meeting a goal, four factors may be operating singly or together:

(a) The goal is unrealistic; no techniques are known for achieving it.
(b) The organization is applying an inappropriate technique; that is, no matter how well the agency does X, it will not achieve Y because X does not cause Y.
(c) The organization has selected appropriate techniques, but they are implemented improperly.
(d) The organization is appropriately implementing techniques, but the scale is too small to achieve the goal.

If the last reason alone is preventing successful resolution of the problem, policymakers outside of the police department can simply mandate "more of the same" and provide funds to expand current activities. However, if any of the other three factors are operating, then selection of an effective set of solutions requires expertise. City executives and city councils rarely have the expertise to assess the effectiveness of alternative solutions. They could hire staff with such skills, but lacking such staff they should focus their efforts on clarifying the nature of the problems and their priorities among them. If decision makers adopt specific policies that are attempts to do the impossible, then the selection of these policies is no longer an exercise of political accountability but may appropriately be considered political interference.

Political accountability is exercised when decision-makers demand that specific problems be addressed. Identifying which problems are most important should not be left to a police department alone but is properly the substance of policy conflict among all constituencies of a police department. By this definition, two cities could have the same burglary rates, one police department could put little special effort into solving residential burglaries and the other expend great effort, and both departments be equally accountable.

Efficiency is a measurement that compares two or more programs by the value of the inputs into the program against the benefits of the program outputs (Simon, 1976; Whitaker et al., 1980). The term "efficiency" conveys precision, but in policing, the precision is largely illusory. For a number of reasons, efficiency is rarely demanded by the city's citizens or leaders. Among police managers, efficiency is an often used criterion. For support services, such as record keeping or vehicle maintenance, efficiency is subject to fairly accurate measurement because the functions are basically similar to those in business where efficiency measures have long been employed. Unfortunately, on issues of great public concern, such as the reduction of various types of crime, efficiency is both conceptually and practically difficult to measure. When different sides dispute the efficiency of a particular use of police resources, these claims are usually based on impressions, not precise measures.

Equity is another criterion of utmost importance for policing. Everyone can agree that equity has been achieved when similar situations are treated similarly. However, the world is full of situations in which people have honest disagreements about whether two situations are similar, and people frequently disagree on what are equitable ways of treating different situations. Here are three criteria identified by Whitaker and Mastrofsy (1980, 1976), any of which could be employed to define an equitable distribution of service:

    (a)   A single, universal standard. Everyone should receive the same service.
    (b)   A demand criterion. All who ask shall receive.
    (c)   A need criterion. Those who are less advantaged should receive more.

Among competing definitions of equity, groups with divergent positions can claim that their particular solutions are the equitable ones. In general, the decisions in public forums, such as budget hearings, do not address issues of equity. Neighborhoods and interest groups tend to argue for their own pet projects without attention to how other groups fare. The city executive is more likely to employ some notion of equity based on a concern for the welfare of the city as a whole. The police manager, too, is in an excellent position to develop and apply consistent criteria of equity.

Fiscal accountability is maintained through a set of routine controls over the expenditures of public money. Auditors have well-developed techniques to detect abuses ranging from the trivial, such as borrowing from one account to pay bills in another, to the serious, such as stealing for personal gain. Contracts with kickbacks are by far the major drain on public treasuries. Because over 90 percent of police budgets are for salaries and related fringe benefits, opportunities for corrupt contracts are limited. When a police department is corrupt, most of the illegal money is extorted directly from the public and thus falls outside this narrow criterion of fiscal accountability. Because fiscal integrity is by and large well established in the management of police departments, fiscal performance will be excluded from this discussion. Competition among city agencies for larger shares of the municipal budget are not questions of fiscal integrity but questions of priorities, which are properly decided by political direction.

Various combinations of these criteria may be applied to a specific policy. Standards for judging whether a particular policy advances accountability or constitutes interference are summarized here. A policy directive to a police department is an exercise of political accountability to the extent that it is legal, addresses attention to the problem without imposing a solution, is not grossly inefficient, is equitable by some standard, and does not defy fiscal accountability. The less a policy directive meets any of these criteria, the stronger the political interference.

Setting policies for a police department is considerably more complex than this discussion has thus far indicated because attention has been limited to one policy at a time. Because departments are following multiple policies directed toward multiple goals and also because the policies followed to achieve some goals make other goals harder to achieve, the likelihood of conflict is high. An abstract framework needs to be proven against the facts of political life.

POLITICAL VOLATILITY IN
AN EASTERN CITY

The site for applying these criteria is Troy, New York, an old working-class town of 55,000 that has experienced a long-term decline in its industrial base and a consequent loss of population at the rate of 1 percent a year over the last 2 decades. Higher education is now the largest employer. Troy has higher than average unemployment rates, a substantial number of families living below the poverty line, and a high municipal tax effort. The 5 percent of the population that are black live mostly in a deteriorating neighborhood adjoining the central business district. The people are proud of their city and identify strongly with their neighborhoods.

During the first half of this century, Troy was governed by a strong mayor and council form of government dominated by the county Republican party. Mismanagement by the Democrats, who had won control in 1956, spurred various good government groups to ally with the Republicans to pass a referendum in 1960 on a new city charter establishing a city manager form of government to take effect in 1964. The formal arrangements in the charter are standard. The city manager serves at the pleasure of the city council and exercises all executive powers, including authority to appoint and dismiss. The council's authority to set basic policy and pass legislation brings it into conflict with the city manager on where to draw the line between policy and implementation. The council majority selects a mayor from among their number to preside over meetings.

The first city manager, a professional from out of state, chose to resign quietly in his third year rather than obey the order of the county Republican party to promote a particular police sergeant to captain. The second city manager made the promotion, arranged kickbacks to the county Republicans from contractors doing business with the city, and held office for seventeen months until forced out by a state criminal investigation. The third, a professor of management from a local college, served eleven months before being replaced by a professional city manager recruited from outside. This fourth manager had dominated a city council split four-to-three Republican until the Democrats attained control of all seats through their 1971 election victory. He attributed his stormy firing in early 1972 to his refusal to obey the Democratic county chairman's direct demand to place Democrats in appointed city positions then held by Republicans. John P. Buckley, an engineer native to the city, stepped from the head of a city department to acting city manager. Confirmed after some months, Buckley served a fractious council. The Republican majority fired him in mid-1977. After the Democrats won all four council seats in the November 1977 election on the strength of their campaign slogan, "Bring Back Buckley," he consolidated his power, and Democrats continued their substantial majority on the council.

The typology of municipal politics developed by Oliver Williams has a category that aptly fits Troy—arbitrator government (Williams, 1961). The other categories are the provider of amenities, the booster where growth is the priority, and the caretaker where low taxation is the priority. In arbitrator government, energies are consumed in conflicts. Whenever a policy question arises, it immediately becomes a partisan issue as one party takes one side in an effort to derive some narrow advantage, and the other party swings to the opposition for the same reasons. The volatility of Troy's elections is promoted by the large proportion of voters registered without party affiliation, 43 percent compared to 33 percent Republicans and 22 percent Democrats as of 1975.

The police department of 125 officers in 1973 had had no coherent policy direction since at least 1956 when the Democrats had elevated a patrolman directly to chief. Although he had scored lowest of 7 on the examination, he became promotable under the civil service rule of 3 when men ahead of him on the list were removed through receiving other promotions. Civil service tenure then froze him into the chief's position, but he never learned management. The captain of detectives, a Republican, had had dictatorial control over his 33-man unit and also drafted departmental orders for issuance by the succession of Republicans who served as part-time commissioners of public safety.

Now comes a long tale of accountability and interference covering the operation of three mechanisms for controlling municipal police: selection of the police manager, election of city officials, and city council directives.

ACCOUNTABILITY THROUGH APPOINTMENT OF A POLICE MANAGER

A choice of managers provides the best opportunity to set new policy directions, whether in the world of business or government. The city executive's power to hire and fire a police manager creates an overall political accountability through selection of an individual whose exercise of internal accountability creates policies that are legal, effective, efficient, equitable, and fiscally honest. The studies by the IACP and the Police Foundation in the mid-1970s suggest careful weighing of the candidates' abilities and the city's and the department's needs in the selection of a new head (IACP, 1976; Kelly, 1975). The events in the appointment and reappointment of George O'Connor as commissioner of public safety illustrate total lack of reasoned public participation in the selection and give examples of decisions entangled in other conflicts. Briefly, in 1972 a management study funded by LEAA and conducted by a national consulting firm precipitated the retirement of the chief. City Manager Buckley asked the consultants to recommend a professional, traveled to Washington to interview their nominee, and offered him the position. O'Connor accepted without visiting the city. When Buckley announced the appointment, the newspapers featured the consultants' blast at the department. Given everyone's ignorance of the new commissioner, the fearful leadership of the Patrolmen's Benevolent Association circulated rumors that this outsider was a hatchet man. Commissioner O'Connor immediately stressed his intention to work with all members of the department while criticizing department operating practices as belonging in the Smithsonian.

The second opportunity for public debate on overall direction of the department occurred when O'Connor made nine promotions in May 1973 but left the chief's position vacant. The PBA immediately took the commissioner to court to force appointment of a chief. In July, the county judge ruled that filling the vacancy was discretionary because the city charter stated that "the Commissioner of Public Safety *may* appoint a police chief." The city charter revision commission accepted a watered down version of O'Connor's proposal that the commissioner have professional qualifications but, contrary to his recommendation, changed the language to "shall appoint a police chief." After the voters approved the referendum in November, the commissioner, with the concurrence of the city manager, appointed the chief from the top of the civil service list.

The next opportunity for public debate on overall leadership of the department occurred after O'Connor informed Buckley in the summer of 1975 that he would be resigning to take a position in Washington. The city manager delayed making the resignation public until after O'Connor had left in September. Buckley had no intention of filling the commissioner's position, leaving the chief to run the department.

The 1975 election, however, produced three new council members who obtained all the seats on the council's public safety committee. The one Democrat was a professor of political science who aspired to bring back strong mayor government and to be elected mayor.

In January 1976, the committee began an active interest in many aspects of department management. In March, the murder of a 75-year-old woman brought 100 citizens to a meeting of the council's public safety committee. The committee formally ordered Buckley to appoint a commissioner within 6 days. The choice was a former official of the state corrections commission who had campaigned for the Republican council candidates the previous fall. Buckley promised to meet the deadline, but when the favorite declined, he managed to avoid making the appointment. In November, the failure of voters to favor either of the charter amendments that abolished the commissioner position rekindled the council's ambition to fill it. When the council by a 4 to 3 vote inserted the position into the 1977 budget, Buckley again offered George O'Connor the commissionership. O'Connor accepted as his work in Washington had ended, and he was engaged in private consulting. He and his family had not relocated from the house purchased 3 years earlier. At the regular January council meeting, the city manager replied to a councilman's question that he was working on filling the commissioner's position. He notified council members by letter 2 days later that he intended to reappoint O'Connor. Enraged at this failure to consult them, a 6 to 1 majority of the council voted at their February meeting to put a referendum on the November ballot to abolish the position and to change the police chief and fire chief into department heads who serve at the pleasure of the city manager. The March council meeting included the public hearing on the referendum but only one citizen spoke, testifying that an outside commissioner was necessary.

The referendum on police leadership was pushed to a back burner in July when the Republican majority of the council fired the city manager, and the Democrats eventually turned the firing into the main campaign issue. In September, the commissioner had written the League of Women Voters offering to assist any inquiry or discussion on the governance of the public safety function, but the League only belatedly opposed the referendum on its wording. The issue surfaced in late October when a newspaper story reported that the police union's vote at its monthly meeting was running about 19 to 10 for abolishing the commissioner's position. Because all ranks belonged to the union, a captain then collected signatures on a petition from 65 members opposing the union vote and specifically endorsing the retention of civil service tenure for the police chief. Note how the union leadership had phrased its stand as an attack on the commissioner, whereas the membership petition was phrased as protection for the chief, although the issues were two sides of a single coin. When the union leaders refused the captain's request to hold a second membership vote on the issue, he made public the stand of the majority of officers against a "political head of the police department." The lone councilman outspoken for preserving the commissioner's post was not up for election. He observed that the referendum had been transformed from selecting governance structures into a vote on whether George O'Connor was doing a good job. His interpretation was supported by the few letters to the editor from citizens that urged abolishing the post in order to remove O'Connor. The Friday before the election, the 11:00 p.m. television news covered the issue by interviewing Commissioner O'Connor. The same day, the city's newspaper urgently opposed the referendum on the grounds that a commissioner is essential to prevent political interference in the police and fire departments and to protect elected officials from the power of the unions. Most people were completely uninformed on the issue. Of the 17,000 voters for city council seats, less than 60 percent voted on the referendum, and they defeated it 2 to 1.

In 1983, the issue of selecting a department head again arose due to the unexpected death of the chief. His vigor at age 45 had given most command officers a reason not to bother taking the civil service examination for chief, and only the newest captain had passed it. Because the captain was one of the most capable members of the department, the selection of a new chief was the simple matter of promoting the only person on the list. As the institutional arrangements now stand, a police chief is mandatory, must be selected from within the department according to civil service procedures, and has tenure. The city manager retains the discretion to appoint and dismiss commissioners or to leave the position vacant.

One city's use of the most powerful instrument of political accountability has been examined in some detail in order to illustrate some problems in its use. First, if the city executive withholds information from the city council and the public, then the accountability of the police department stops with the executive and does not carry over to those who may represent the diverse voices of the people. During the two decisions to select a commissioner, the city manager consulted no representatives of the public. Second, changes in institutional arrangements may be made for reasons completely irrelevant to accountability issues. The police union forced the appointment of a chief in 1973 in order to obtain a promotional position. In 1977, the city council, locked in a power struggle with the city manager, attempted to cut a police leadership position as a blow to the city manager, quite apart from the merits of the issue. Third, direction of the department can change hands without any debate or effort to create debate on the performance standards the public expects. Fourth, when the head of the police department must be selected from the inside, the small size of the talent pool makes luck a large factor.

ELECTIONS STIR CONFUSION
WITHOUT PROVIDING ACCOUNTABILITY

The studies in recent years of public concern over crime and police protection have shown that these issues are tailor made for politicians aspiring to office and ill-suited to incumbents, who obviously have not "solved" the crime problem (Finckenauer, 1978; Buffum and Sagi, 1983; McPherson, 1983; and Guyot, 1983). Scheingold (1984) has argued persuasively that fear of crime gives salience to the punitive strand of American culture that yearns for simple "cops and robbers" solutions, as on television. The decade of election campaigns in the city under examination fits so perfectly this pattern of the outs demanding action that a quick summary of the events is in order.

Crime became an issue in the city in May 1975. The third murder of the year on the north side touched off citizen protests against a crime wave. The city council voted five to two along party lines to hire ten more officers, against the advice of the commissioner and city manager. The voters, also displeased over the gaping holes where urban renewal had stalled, defeated the three incumbent Democrats while electing one Democratic and three Republican newcomers. In 1977 the Democrats won all four seats after they refocused their campaign in mid-October from developing the central business district to reinstating the city manager. The 1979 campaign had almost no issues, both parties vying for credit for the city's development. One incumbent from each party ran and won, while the addition of two Democratic newcomers continued the six-to-one Democratic majority.

In 1981, the Republicans seized upon foot patrol and keeping the department fully staffed as two major issues. The local daily ran a seven-part series on police manpower, painting a picture of an under-staffed department. The Democratic council majority moved quickly to deprive the Republicans of the police issue by asking the state to conduct a study on the feasibility of foot patrol. The mayor also proposed an advisory committee to explore the possibility of establishing a neighborhood watch program. The Democrats won all four seats. In 1982 a charter referendum supported by the Republicans won by a huge margin. It overhauled the council to provide only three at-large seats and six new district seats. In the 1983 campaign, candidates for the six district seats were grasping for issues and found crime. One Republican hopeful took this stand in his election flyer:

> In the beginning I was concerned about crime. Then I became frightened. The more homes I visit, the more crimes I find have been committed. I am no longer frightened. I am angry—"mad as hell" is more appropriate. I cannot fault our police officers, who are under-staffed and who have one hand tied behind their backs. They share your frustration, CITY HALL does not. The Commissioner of Public Safety stated at a public meeting in the YMCA on September 8, "It is the City's policy to reduce crime to a tolerable level." You have my pledge that policy will change, and change fast! . . . Let's all get angry together. THERE IS NO *TOLERABLE LEVEL* OF CRIME.

The police union, which had endorsed some candidates in previous years, decided to forgo endorsement but to hold a public forum inviting all candidates to address the issues of crime and adequacy of police staffing. Twelve candidates agreed that the city needed more police officers, but when specifically asked where they would find the funds, none bit the bullet of higher tax rates. On the Sunday before the election, the union ran an ad proclaiming no confidence in Commissioner O'Connor. The voters, however, elected five out of six Democrats, thus supporting the city manager who supported the commissioner. The candidate who attacked the commissioner for tolerating crime lost by a larger margin than any other Republican or Democrat.

This sequence of six council elections interspersed with two referendums provides not one example of informed debate on police issues. The events do provide examples of political interference through attempts to campaign on specific solutions. The least sensible campaign stand taken by a party endorsed candidate occurred in 1983 after a decade of effort by the police manager to increase public understanding. The candidate's message that there is no tolerable level of crime has the implication that police officers with their hands untied could wipe out crime. Here is a clear example of a department decried as ineffective because the goal is unrealistic.

One major conclusion that the events here support is that the crime issue is perfectly tailored for the party out of power. Because any level of any crime can be considered too much, the opposition can point to the ineffectiveness of the incumbents' policies and promise to take decisive action. The specific promises are often more manpower, "a more of the same solution" that is likely to be less effective than alternative approaches. A second conclusion is that campaigning on fear of crime is not a sure way to win office. During two campaigns that focused most on police issues, 1981 and 1983, the minority party won a total of two seats out of the ten contested. Part of the explanation may be that voters had no serious dissatisfaction with current police service.

INTERFERENCE AND ACCOUNTABILITY EXERCISED BY THE CITY COUNCIL

This description of city council policymaking for police traces the origin in a wave of fear and covers three intensely active years. A fundamental reason that the council was particularly active in police affairs during 1976-1978 was that the executive was weak. Everyone believed that Commissioner O'Connor had left for good in September 1975. The chief attempted to handle problems quietly inside the department while denying information to the press and consequently received a bad press. Within the department, he referred to the council members as the enemy. The council found ways to harass him, such as taking away his city car when he moved to a house out of town. O'Connor's return in January 1977 gave strength to the department, but by then Buckley was suffering severe attacks from the four-to-three Republican majority, culminating in his firing in August 1977. The new acting city manager could not gain cooperation from key city hall employees and was out of his element in dealing with the city unions.

Council policies on police matters listed in Table 6.1 show the application of the criteria distinguishing political accountability from

TABLE 6.1
Judgment of City Council Policies as Acts of
Accountability or Interference

Year	Issue	Judgment	Grounds for Judgment
1975	Ten more officers	I	Ineffective, not a problem of scale.
1976	Directing department attention to charges of excessive force	A	Set priority.
1976	Council to read internal affairs files	I	Personnel matter.
1976	Foot patrol	I	Ineffective, X does not cause Y.
1976	Shotguns in patrol cars	I	Ignored effect on other priorities.
1977	Community relations board	A	Create new communications channel.
1977	Downtown safety and four other problems	A	Effectiveness, set priorities.
1977	Five solutions to problems	I	Ignored effect on other priorities.
1977	Ten operational directives	I	Ineffective, no service goals.
1975-77	Neighborhood police station	I	Ineffective, X does not cause Y. Equity not addressed.
1977	Cut budget 5%	A	Global priority between services and taxes.
1978	Hearing on team policing	I	Ineffective, confused service goals.
1977-83	More foot patrol	I	Ineffective, not a problem of scale.

A = Act of political accountability.
I = Act of political interference.

interference. Accountability is a judgment that a political body should make the decision; it is not an endorsement of the contents of the decision.

In May 1975, public attention snapped crime into focus. Previously, there had been unease about burglaries, vandalism, and some muggings near the high school. A wave of fear surged when a high school boy murdered his friend; more than 200 citizens poured out to a previously planned neighborhood meeting with the commissioner. People demanded action. One candidate circulated a petition that the county sheriff patrol the neighborhood. The solutions poured forth: more police, attack dogs, a neighborhood police station, unmarked cars, auxiliary police. The PBA president endorsed the call for ten more officers. O'Connor questioned whether the additional manpower would have a noticeable effect on crime. He explained that the misbehavior of youth was the primary cause for concern and suggested that the money might be better spent on recreation programs, youth centers, or employment training. The city council, however, directed the hiring of ten more officers against the explicit advice of the commissioner and the city manager. When O'Connor brought forward his plan for coping with the fears, a citizens' crime prevention council, it passed the city council due only to the absence of two members of the majority and was rejected at the state level.

Throwing manpower at crime is an automatic solution, a reflex action. In this situation, the city council started with the vague notion that "crime has increased" and provided the vague solution of hiring more officers to do whatever it is they are supposed to do. This action was interference. In broader perspective, more manpower can be an appropriate means deliberately chosen to address a specific crime problem. For instance, a patrol captain may assign an officer to foot patrol in the central business district during the Christmas shopping season with the knowledge that purse snatching can be expected to rise at this season and with the aim of using visible police presence to reassure shoppers and deter purse snatchers. A sergeant may work with his squad to increase surveillance of a school parking lot where a rash of vandalism is occurring. However, when crime problems are only vaguely recognized, then the solutions cannot be definite. When the leadership of a city decides to expand the police force, the hidden implication is that the additional officers will not solve the problem because the additional positions were not created as temporary positions but will continue into the indefinite future. The immediate difficulty with hiring as the solution to a current crime problem is that rarely will less than six months elapse before the new officers are out on patrol.

The public safety committee of the council was the source of council policy on police issues. The councilwoman elected in November, 1975, who was soon to chair the committee, began to consider policy issues even before she took office. At her suggestion, the *Times Record* published a brief questionnaire for citizens to clip and return that asked about the adequacy of police and fire protection, the need for foot patrol, and willingness to pay for more protection. The December 30, 1975, news story covering 50 replies to the survey began, "By a four-to-one margin, residents are not happy with their police department." One citizen's comment, that 70 percent of the officers were drinkers, particularly riled the union leaders. After the editor had refused to print a retraction, the PBA filed a $10 million libel suit against the paper.

In the city council, the newcomers tended to cooperate, in effect the one new Democrat giving support to the slim Republican majority. The public safety committee worked as a team to probe into the performance of the police department. On January 1, a six-column story describing two arrests in which officers had employed force prompted the council committee to inquire whether the force had been excessive and whether the department had whitewashed the incidents. By mid-January, the Democrat on the committee persuaded the Republicans to expand the inquiry by meeting with union members to hear their views on department management in general. The committee then pressed to obtain internal affairs records, a move widely interpreted as a fishing expedition. Buckley refused on the grounds that the records were exempt from the sunshine law. When the public safety committee persisted, the PBA obtained a court injunction. In sum, the council's directing departmental attention to excessive force complaints was setting priorities, clearly an exercise of accountability, but the attempt to read the internal affairs files was interference in personnel matters, damaging to internal accountability.

The need for foot patrol was a frequent note during this period, voiced by individual citizens, citizen groups, and council members. The chief was adamant that foot patrol was an anachronism and refused to make any assignments beyond the usual posting of a foot officer downtown during the Christmas shopping season. Because the chair of the public safety committee was the owner of a downtown coffee shop, she was particularly aware of the downtown merchants' desire for walking officers.

Residents of the north end of town had been expressing a desire for a precinct station because the murder there had created the wave of fear. Because neighboring Albany had been operating a storefront as the headquarters for their single neighborhood police team, the request for a local building had become entwined with a request for team policing in that neighborhood.

The city manager and police chief eased the pressure for change on three fronts by proposing that expert advice be sought from the police training bureau in Albany on appropriate departmental discipline, team policing, and the vacant commissioner's position. In September 1976, the state agency provided three reports answering the questions the way the police chief desired. The reports went on the shelf because they had already served their purpose of cooling the council.

Union leaders initiated a formal request to the city council in late 1976, the first in four years. Three PBA officials met with the public safety committee over officer safety and obtained an order to the chief to place shotguns in the cars. O'Connor returned to the commissionership before this order was implemented and ordered that the shotguns be placed in the sergeants' patrol van and only after officers had received training in their use. This command, "Do X!" was interference. If the council had directed the city manager to develop means to increase the safety of officers even at the risk of increased shooting of citizens, this would be an exercise of accountability. The advantage of switching a policy discussion from focus on a single means to the trade-offs among ends is that the broad consequences of a policy become clearer.

In early November the city council proposed a police community relations board. The chief immediately opposed it on the grounds that it could become a civilian review board. This council initiative was an exercise of accountability whether it was to open a new channel of communication or to empower a separate review function. The intrinsic difficulty of reviewing police exercises of discretion is that the operation of a civilian review board is likely to interfere with internal accountability to the police manager.

When O'Connor resumed the commissionership in January 1977, the public safety committee presented him with a list of 27 items, 21 pertaining to police and the rest to firefighting. One item asked for legislative and budgetary recommendations. There were 5 items that called attention to service problems: protection for the central business district, snow removal and parking, traffic safety, and community relations. There were 5 that were suggested solutions to service problems, such as meter maids issuing tickets for littering and a team policing grant for the north end of town. A total of 10 items concerned operational direction of the department: revival of the narcotics division and the scuba team, the system of vehicle maintenance, the shift detectives work, and the like. O'Connor met for 2 hours with the committee and 2 additional councilmen going over his decisions for each of the items. The council accepted his decisions. As part of his plan for downtown safety, he created a regular walking post, a clear case of accountability because the council set the priorities, and the commissioner developed the specific means. The council's solutions to five problems would have been interference if they had imposed them. Likewise, their 10 operational directives were commands to "Do X!" but without any connection to service priorities. For the next months, pressures on the police department eased as the council majority directed its attentions to criticizing the city manager.

As the 1977 election season warmed, the issue of a storefront police station for the north side reemerged. The woman who in 1975 had organized a citizens group in the neighborhood decided to run for city council. When she approached Buckley with a plan for a storefront police station staffed by nonsworn personnel, he and O'Connor agreed. The Democrats unveiled their plan at a press conference. The Republican councilwoman who had been pressing for a storefront for fifteen months learned of it in the newspaper. The *Times Record*, ordinarily highly supportive of the city manager, agreed editorially with the councilwoman's accusation that his motives "were totally political." Buckley had slapped a strong-willed councilwoman at the same time that Republicans were receiving results from a privately commissioned opinion poll that indicated he was not popular. Given this impetus, the Republicans fired him.

Commissioner O'Connor presented a plan to the acting city manager in September for three public safety service centers to be located in fire stations and to be open afternoons and early evenings. The staff member at each center, paid through CETA funds, would offer information on crime prevention, fire prevention, dog licensing, and social services, would register dogs, bicycles, and valuables, and would receive citizen complaints. The centers would serve as locations for meetings with police officers and would remind people of the presence of safety forces in their neighborhoods. The councilwoman and the citizens' group from the north side liked the plan so well that they incorporated it into their storefront proposal but retained their original ideas for assigning two juvenile officers and two additional police cars there.

In early October, O'Connor told the acting city manager that he was taking on the councilwoman to prevent inequitable allocation of police personnel to the north side and to prevent the assignment of police officers to man the center. Either the city manager should stay out of the fight or fire him. The acting city manager did neither. The plan as implemented placed the captain in charge of the crime prevention unit working out of the center three days a week. O'Connor's explanation appearing in the *Times Record* was that the captain's assignment was not a concession to the union and the citizens group but rather was done to satisfy citizens' desire for a larger uniformed police presence. The captain would be of sufficient rank to make the police patrols respond to a problem brought to him at the center. O'Connor also changed two detective assignments from generalist to juvenile, salving a sore point of police officers and some citizens unhappy over his abolishing the juvenile unit six months earlier. As O'Connor had predicted, the center was a lonely place, averaging two visitors a day. Because the police business that can be conducted from inside a building is providing information and channeling requests for service, the telephone makes local centers unnecessary.

Election day came and went, the Democrats sweeping all seats on the promise to restore the city manager. The rump session had the responsibility of levying higher taxes to pay for costs incurred through inflation and previously negotiated contracts. In a quiet decision, the council chose to cut 5 percent from every departmental budget. This police department, like many, allocated 95 percent of the budget to personnel, 3 percent to supplies, 2 percent to contractual services, and 1 percent to equipment. The only source of a substantial saving was personnel. The commissioner chose to give up the 9 vacant police officer positions, thus reducing the department's authorized sworn strength to the level before the furor over crime. Amid the drama of the change in council majorities and city managers, this important policy decision was unnoticed. The council was exercising accountability in deciding not to raise taxes, however unwise in failing to set priorities among services to be cut.

The struggle over team policing had already started before the end of 1977, making the episode over the storefront into a preliminary test of strength. During the summer of 1979, O'Connor had persuaded Buckley that his long considered plan for changing the structure of the department to team policing was right for Troy. The telling argument was that team policing would place more men on the street. In July, O'Connor submitted an application for a $74,000, 18 months' extension of the current LEAA crime prevention grant to plan and then implement neighborhood team policing throughout the city in April, 1978. The 6 objectives were to increase citizens' sense of personal safety, citizen cooperation with officers and participation in setting neighborhood priorities, departmental coordination, command personnel's contribution to department operations, investigative effectiveness, especially for crimes against the person, and the productivity of individual officers by enhancing personal commitment and developing greater peer concern. The means to accomplish all this was to restructure the delivery of service so that primary coordination took place on a geographic rather than shift basis. A part-time resident coordinator for each team would work out of his or her home to facilitate communication with the community and among team members. Officers at all levels would be involved in the planning, and, after implementation, monthly team meetings would address local problems. The largest budget item, $36,000, was for police overtime for the planning task forces and the team meetings.

A change machine, a term Egon Bittner and Herman Goldstein coined to describe the $5,000,000 Police Foundation project with the Dallas PD, aptly labels the police union perception of team policing. A change machine is a highly publicized process of change promoted by outside experts and outside funds. The development of a large evaluation gave credence to the union's depiction of team policing as an alien instrument. Initially, the author had designed an evaluation costing $700, but the availability of LEAA funds set aside for intensive evaluation provided an attractive opportunity. The final design was a 2-year evaluation employing extensive survey research at a total cost of $500,000 in LEAA funds.

Commissioner O'Connor had distributed a copy of his team policing proposal to every member of the department when the action grant was submitted, but few had commented. An underlying source of officer discontent was that the PBA contract had run 1975-1976, but the terms of the new contract were in binding arbitration, finally announced on May 12, 1978. When the PBA held its 1977 fall election of officers, the leaders polled membership opinion with a signup sheet headed, "Team policing, yes or no." The sheet obtained 90 no's and not one yes. O'Connor proceeded with the planning by offering all members opportunities to participate in task forces with overtime compensation for the time invested. Initially, only eighteen officers signed up. The union leadership decided that only a watch dog committee should attend, without participating. One young, highly respected officer who had not understood the message went to a meeting and gained the reputation of hurting the men, a canard that took several months to live down.

The union success with the city council in obtaining air conditioned cars at the time they demanded shotguns had given them confidence that they could find allies in the council without provoking types of political interference they opposed, such as the demand for internal

affairs files. A city council legislative hearing was the climax of the union's campaign against team policing. The drama was held on two consecutive evenings in early April. Eloquent testimony that team policing would ruin a good department was presented by fifteen officers. The council deliberated a week and decided five to two, Democrats against Republicans, that the commissioner should proceed with team policing on a trial basis and decide jointly with the union whether to permit the evaluation. In response to this adverse decision, about fifty off-duty police officers picketed city hall and distributed leaflets criticizing the city council for playing partisan politics in disregard of the security needs of the community. Their specific criticisms of team policing were that it equaled the elimination of a narcotics unit, the stripping of the detective bureau, the elimination of the traffic department, and the stripping of the juvenile bureau. The union directly accused the council and the city manager of not listening to the people. Within the department, the union leadership and the chief pressured officers and command staff to ostracize the commissioner, with considerable success. Meanwhile, the complexity of the evaluation grant had slowed LEAA's preparation of the grant contracts, which finally arrived in early July. The city manager refused to sign them, ending the evaluation.

Team policing operated all summer while some members of the department felt rancor and others despaired that the struggle had not yet ended between the commissioner and the union. O'Connor kept close watch on all indicators of productivity, noting that output on easily measurable performance such as response time and arrests had remained good. At the end of the summer, the commissioner developed a replacement for team policing worked out with the city manager, the chief, and the captains. In September after O'Connor announced the termination of team policing, he said flatly in a television interview that political interference had taken place and that he had been disappointed that community groups had not been more active in support of team policing. All parties to the conflict cooled down and eventually resumed good working relationships. Stung by union criticisms, city council members put some distance between themselves and union concerns. The city manager exercised more power vis-à-vis the council because the Democratic majority continued to be elected on their pledge to support him. Neither the scope nor the intensity of council policymaking for police has recurred in this city. Since 1981, the new chairman of the council public safety committee has explicitly left operational questions to the professionals.

CONCLUSIONS

Three generalizations help to explain the predominance of political interference over political accountability during the three years of intense activity. Out of the fourteen issues characterized in Table 6.1, the police union supported none of the four acts of accountability. Conversely, of the ten acts of interference, the union instigated or actively supported six and opposed only one. The hottest battle, over team policing, would not have occurred without union action. The three generalizations are as follows:

(1) The smallness of the attentive public for police affairs and the episodic nature of attention by a broader public leave the stage to police management and the police union.
(2) In the public debate on policies, the union and the police manager usually stake out the two sides to issues.
(3) The larger the number of citizens participating in a policy decision, the more likely the union is to win and the police manager to lose.

Many other mechanisms exist for policymaking by agencies outside police departments that have not received attention here. The city executive is the major source of policy direction from outside the department. Union contracts often set policy in ways that interfere dramatically with internal accountability, such as seniority rights to positions, minimum manning, and maintenance of standards clauses. The budget process is little used to set priorities because program budgeting has not been adopted. Some civil service commissions and personnel departments exercise great power over position definition, personnel selection, and promotion. In addition, the specialized review processes, such as the Seattle audit to review political intelligence gathering and civilian review boards, may be used. Prosecutors and courts routinely review the legality of arrests. Federal and state civil suits are brought with increasing frequency as a means of forcing particular policy decisions. The tests of interference and accountability developed here appear useful in judging these exercises of power as well.

REFERENCES

BUFFUM, P. C. and R. SAGI (1983) "Philadelphia: The politics of reform and retreat," in A. Heinz et al. (eds.) Crime in City Politics. New York: Longman.

FINCKENAUER, J. O. (1978) "Crime as a national political issue: 1964-76: From law and order to domestic tranquility." Crime and Delinquency (January): 13-27.

GOLDSTEIN, H. (1977) Policing a Free Society. Cambridge, MA: Ballinger.

GUYOT, D. (1983) "Newark: Crime and politics in a declining city," in A. Heinz et al. (eds.) Crime in City Politics. New York: Longman.

HREBINIAK, L. G. (1978) Complex Organizations. St. Paul, MN: West.

International Association of Chiefs of Police [IACP] (1976) The Police Chief Executive Report. Washington, DC: U.S. Government Printing Office.

KELLY, M. J. (1975) Police Chief Selection: A Handbook for Local Government. Washington, DC: The Police Foundation and the International City Management Association.

McPHERSON, M. (1983) "Minneapolis: Crime in a politically fragmented arena," in A. Heinz et al. (eds.) Crime in City Politics. New York: Longman.

O'CONNOR, G. W. (1976) "Some not so random thoughts on police improvement." Troy, NY: Department of Public Safety.

SCHEINGOLD, S. A. (1984) The Politics of Law and Order. New York: Longman.

SIMON, H. A. (1976) Administrative Behavior: A Study of Decision Making Processes in Administrative Organizations. New York: The Free Press.

WASSERMAN, R. (1977) "The governmental setting," in B. L. Garmire (ed.) Local Government Police Management. Washington, DC: International City Management Association.

WHITAKER, G. P. and S. D. MASTROFSKI (1976) "Equity in the delivery of police services." Presented at the annual meeting of the Southern Political Science Association, 1976.

——— E. OSTROM, R. B. PARKS, and S. L. PERCY (1980) Measuring Police Performance (Report prepared under grant number 78-NI-AY-0086 from the National Institute of Justice). Bloomington, IN: Workshop in Political Theory and Policy Analysis.

WILLIAMS, O. (1961) "A typology for comparative local government." Midwest Journal of Politics 5 (May): 150-164.

7.

THE POLITICS OF POLICE ACCOUNTABILITY:
The Seattle Police Spying Ordinance as a Case Study

Samuel Walker

University of Nebraska at Omaha

In 1979 the Seattle, Washington, City Council enacted a municipal ordinance to regulate intelligence gathering by the Seattle Police Department.[1] The law was the outgrowth of revelations in 1974 that the Seattle police had maintained intelligence files on an estimated 750 local citizens. The subjects of these files ranged from black and Hispanic community leaders to prominent Republican politicians, including one assistant U.S. attorney. The campaign to control police misconduct was led by the Coalition on Government Spying (COGS), a coalition of over 40 community groups, with the active support of one key member of the Seattle City Council.[2]

The Seattle Police Intelligence Ordinance represents a unique approach to the control of police misconduct (Paulsen, 1970; Potts, 1983). Over the past decade, revelations of illegal police spying have occurred in New York City, Chicago, Los Angeles, Memphis, and by the Michigan State Police and the F.B.I. (Center for National Security Studies [CNSS], 1981; U.S. Senate, 1976). "Illegal" spying, in this context, refers to police maintaining intelligence files on persons and/or organizations who are not suspected of any criminal activity. The subjects of this illegal spying have generally sought recourse through the courts, seeking civil damages and/or court-ordered controls over police misconduct. Seattle is the only instance of legislatively enacted controls. The Seattle ordinance takes on larger significance with respect to the F.B.I. It has been offered as a model for a legislative "charter" for the bureau (U.S. House of Representatives, 1979) although, ironically, it is based on a model proposed for control of the F.B.I. in the first place (Berman, 1976; Revelle, 1979).

This chapter examines the nature and impact of the Seattle Police Intelligence Ordinance. It reviews the essential features of the law and its impact during its first four years. Particular attention is given to the operations of the auditor, the process for monitoring compliance with the law.

ESSENTIAL FEATURES

The purpose of the Seattle police intelligence ordinance is "to permit the collection and recording of information for law enforcement purposes," while at the same time protecting the rights of citizens guaranteed by both the U.S. and Washington constitutions. These include traditional First Amendment rights and the right to privacy. To achieve this balance, the ordinance contains three essential features: a definition of restricted activity, civil penalties, and a monitoring mechanism.

Restricted Activity

The Seattle ordinance restricts three activities of the Seattle Police Department: the collection of information pertaining to a citizen's political, religious, or private sexual matters; the use of police infiltrators and informants; and the disclosure of nonpublic police information.

There are two categories of information subject to restriction. The category of "restricted information" includes information about:

(i) an individual's political or religious associations, activities, beliefs, or opinions; political or religious associations, activities, beliefs, or opinions; (ii) the political or religious activities, beliefs, or opinions and the membership, mailing, subscription, or contributor lists of a political or religious organization, an organization formed for the protection or advancement of civil rights or civil liberties, or an organization formed for community purposes; or (iii) an individual's membership or participation in such an organization, or in a demonstration for community purposes [Seattle City Council, 1979. See note 1].

The category of "private sexual information," meanwhile, includes "any information about a person's sexual practices or orientation" (see note 1).

The law does not prohibit the collection of such information but only regulates collection and usage. Private sexual information, for example, may be collected if "the information involves a reported or observed sex crime," and in three other situations related to criminal activity. Restricted political and religious information may be collected "if the subject of the information is reasonably suspected of criminal activity or the information relates to the reliability of a victim or witness" (see note 1).

Regulations take several forms. First, the collection of restricted information must be authorized in writing by a supervisor of the rank of lieutenant or above. Such authorizations must contain detailed information about the crime under investigation and expire after ninety days. Written authorizations are not required, however, for the collection of private sexual information. This distinction reflects the recognition "that thousands of cases every year required legitimate collection and use of sexual preference information" (Bernstein, 1979: 86). On this point, members of COGS made a major concession to arguments advanced by law enforcement and prosecutorial members of the ordinance drafting committee.

The issue of protecting visiting dignitaries raised other serious questions. This section of the ordinance was, in the words of City Attorney Bernstein (1979: 100), "especially difficult to draft." Potential threats against the safety of such dignitaries would come, almost by definition, from politically oriented individuals or groups. Investigation of such potential threats would, therefore, come close to violating the letter or the spirit of the ordinance. The resulting compromise follows the form of the general exemptions permitted. The police may collect otherwise restricted information, but it must be maintained in a separate file, may not be collected until the department has official notice that a particular dignitary will visit the city, shall be available only to those officers assigned to dignitary protection, and must be purged within sixty days after collection is authorized.

The ordinance restricts the use of infiltrators and informants. This provision is notable because only a few American law enforcement agencies have developed internal policies governing the use of informants. Infiltration of an organization must be authorized in writing by the chief of police and is permitted only to collect restricted information pursuant to the other provisions of the ordinance. Finally, the chief of police is required to establish procedures for the review of any use of infiltrators. Paid informants are specifically prohibited from participating in unlawful acts of violence, using illegal techniques to obtain information, initiating or planning criminal acts, or participating in criminal activities. An exception to the latter point permits participation where it "is necessary to obtain information needed for purposes of prosecution" (see note 1).

Finally, the ordinance restricts the disclosure of information to five narrowly defined situations.[3] The question of exchanging information with other law enforcement agencies was especially problematic and created the only serious problem in implementing the law (see below).

Civil Penalties

Any person injured by a violation of the ordinance has a cause of action against the City of Seattle for civil damages of $500. An organization subject to illegal infiltration has a cause of action for damages of $1,000. The city is not liable for actions taken by any official acting in good faith, although the meaning of this concept is not specified in detail (Bernstein, 1979). The Coalition on Government Spying originally defined criminal penalties as one of its primary goals but was not able to achieve this provision (Taylor, 1983).

Implementation and Monitoring

Section 35 of the ordinance requires the chief of police to promulgate rules and regulations to guide police department personnel in the conduct of investigations and in the use of informants and infiltrators. The chief promulgated these rules and regulations in a 17-page memo, and all members of the police department received 14 hours of training related to the ordinance (Seattle Police Department, 1979).

The most important provision of the ordinance creates an auditor to monitor compliance with the law at 180-day intervals. The auditor is appointed by the mayor, subject to confirmation by the city council. Somewhat ironically, the concept of an auditor had originated with then Police Chief Hanson in 1975-1976, who proposed it in an effort to avoid legislatively imposed controls (*Seattle Post-Intelligencer*, November 23, 1975; *Seattle Times*, June 6, 1976).

With only five exceptions,[4] the auditor has the power and responsibility to review all police department files. The auditor is specifically required to review each authorization for the collection of restricted information, review other files at random, and all files designated for purging. Following each audit, the auditor is to submit a preliminary report to the chief of police for review and comment and then submit a final report to the mayor and city council. Additionally, the auditor must notify by certified mail any person about whom restricted information had been collected in possible violation of the ordinance.[5]

THE POLICE INTELLIGENCE ORDINANCE
IN ACTION

The following analysis of the Seattle Police Intelligence Ordinance examines it from the perspectives of its supporters, the police department, and the auditor, respectively.

The Supporters' Perspective

From the standpoint of its supporters, the Seattle Police Intelligence Ordinance represents a major victory, with national as well as local significance. The ordinance was based on a proposal originally designed for control of the F.B.I. and is now itself viewed as a model for the control of other local, state, and federal law enforcement agencies (CNSS, 1979).[6]

The ordinance is not regarded as a complete victory, however. Coalition chairperson Kathleen Taylor (1979: 124, 1983) states, "We are not fully satisfied." In their view, the ordinance contains several weaknesses. The collection of restricted information is not prohibited absolutely. Imaginative police officers could easily develop justifications for the collection of restricted information couched in terms that would satisfy the requirements of the law—or at least do so in such a way as to fool the auditor. The good faith defense is a potentially large loophole.[7] The visiting dignitary exemption, meanwhile, allows the collection of restricted information on individuals and groups that would be politically oriented almost by definition. Finally, the ordinance does not contain criminal penalties.

Especially problematic is the potential for willful violations of the ordinance by police officers who conceal restricted information from the auditor. This could easily be accomplished by simply maintaining the files in their personal possession rather than in the department. Precedent for such behavior is ample. J. Edgar Hoover maintained a secret "do not file" set of memos, the existence of which has just come to light. In Los Angeles, detectives hid in a private garage files ordered destroyed by the Los Angeles Police Commission. Gary Marx (1982) puts this problem in a broader context, arguing that the formal rules governing police conduct may only encourage imaginative forms of evasion. Creative evasion of the exclusionary rule has been noted by some observers.

The current auditor concedes that the police could certainly fool him if they really wanted. He adds, however, that the likelihood of this is greatly diminished because of the indirect effects of the ordinance. In his view, the ordinance not only "sensitizes" the police to the importance of respecting the right of privacy but also establishes the principle of openness and scrutiny by outsiders. He also points out that sustaining systematic violations over any length of time without word of them leaking out would be difficult. The fear of such leaks would serve to ensure compliance. In short, the ordinance may have a general deterrent effect on police misconduct (Hoff, 1983).[8]

The Police Perspective

From the standpoint of the Seattle Police Department, the ordinance represents both an unprecedented restriction on investigative techniques traditionally regarded as essential to effective law enforcement and an intrusion by a legislative body into matters long regarded as the exclusive province of law enforcement officials. Also, the law institutionalizes a review of police activities by civilian authorities. Heretofore, police departments have been subject to such outside review only on an ad hoc basis and in extreme situations, usually as a result of litigation or a special investigation growing out of a widely publicized scandal. The Seattle police auditor has the power and authority to inspect all investigative files, not just those pertaining to a particular allegation of police misconduct.

Despite these extraordinary features, the police were unable to prevent enactment of the ordinance. This is particularly surprising when viewed from a national and historical perspective. Police departments have been extremely successful in preventing such intrusions into their activities. The police have been able to mobilize considerable political support, even in the face of scandalous revelations. Elected officials have been reluctant to appear to be "anti-police" (Ruchelman, 1974). Generally lacking detailed knowledge about the administrative and operational aspects of policing, they have been content to take a hands-off approach. The exceptions to this rule are, for the most part, white or black mayors responsive to black constituencies (Juris and Feuille, 1973). Apart from a few recent exceptions, however (Littlejohn, 1981), the police have been able to defeat significant legislative or administrative controls over their activities.

Three factors appear to have undermined political support for the police. First, the well-documented revelations about police spying threw them on the defensive—a position from which they never recovered.[9] Second, the political weakness of the police was compounded by the active participation of one key council member, Mr. Revelle, in support of a restrictive ordinance. Participants agree that the ordinance would not have been passed without his support (Taylor, 1983). Third, participants in the campaign for the ordinance believe that Seattle has a strong tradition of "open government." This tradition, in their opinion, consists of a high degree of participation by the citizenry and a feeling among the citizenry that government should be accountable to the public (Taylor, 1983; Hoff, 1983; Locke, 1983). Whether or not the political culture of Seattle is substantially different from that of other cities is an unverified assertion. Police experts generally concede that differences in "political culture" do exist and that these differences have an important impact on local policing (Wilson, 1973). Nonetheless, the fact that so many participants in the police spying episode feel that Seattle's politics are uniquely "open" suggests that it might have some validity—if only on the basis of W. I. Thomas's (1951: 81) famous maxim, "If men define situations as real they are real in their consequences."[10]

The political context of police issues in Seattle is highly ambiguous, however. In the midst of the police spying controversy, a parallel controversy over the use of deadly force arose. In 1978, Mayor Royer directed the Seattle Police Department to develop new and more restrictive guidelines on when to shoot (*Seattle Times*, December 21, 1977; February 8, 1978; March 30, 1978; May 2, 1978). The police union took the issue to the voters and, by referendum, succeeded in replacing the mayor's restrictive policy with a far more permissive one (*Seattle Times*, April 22, 1978; August 29, 1978; November 8, 1978). The November 1978 election was a political curiosity. Seattle voters approved a resolution opposing forced busing for school integration, voted down an anti-gay rights resolution, and approved the police-sponsored deadly force policy. Thus the police lost political support on the question of spying but not on the use of deadly force. The new deadly force policy essentially permits shooting at fleeing burglary suspects and runs counter to the recent national trend that permits the use of deadly force only in the defense of life (Seattle Police Department, n.d.a.: Section 2.09.030; Geller, 1982).

Despite their basic hostility to the ordinance (Fitzsimons, 1982), members of the police department have apparently complied fully with its letter and spirit.[11] In some respects, they have made an effort to overcomply. Police Chief Fitzsimons permitted the auditor to inspect his personal papers, including items in his safe, despite the fact that the ordinance specifically denies the auditor authority to inspect these materials. The auditor indicated that members of the police department were cordial and cooperative during his initial audit and that the police chief made it clear that he expected full cooperation by all members of the department (Hoff, 1983). In compliance with the ordinance, the police chief developed a seventeen-page memorandum setting forth guidelines for implementing the

ordinance, and all Seattle police officers have received fourteen hours of formal instruction in the content and meaning of the ordinance.

The only serious problem with the ordinance involves police relations with other law enforcement agencies. Because the ordinance opened police files to outside inspection, the Seattle Police Department was expelled from the Law Enforcement Intelligence Unit (LEIU). Additionally, on its own initiative the department did not apply for admission to the Western States Information Network [WSIN] (Ruxlow, 1980). The LEIU is a national organization of police officials that conducts the exchange of criminal intelligence information (U.S. General Accounting Office, 1980). The WSIN is a regional organization sharing information related to narcotics trafficking. Law enforcement officials regard these organizations as means of overcoming the historic fragmentation of American law enforcement. Critics charge that these organizations are unregulated and routinely engage in improper dissemination of information about individuals and organizations engaged in purely political activities (Center for Research on Criminal Justice, 1977).

The ordinance created two specific problems regarding information exchange. First, some information received from the LEIU/WSIN networks would fall with the definition of "restricted information" or "private sexual information." The Seattle police department would violate the law by possessing it. Second, information received from other agencies would be open for inspection by the auditor. This would violate the expectation of the other LEIU/WSIN agencies that the information was confidential.[12]

Following expulsion from LEIU, Seattle police officials argued that the ordinance hindered effective law enforcement (Fitzsimons, 1982). They argued that they could no longer obtain important and necessary information from other law enforcement agencies, particularly about narcotics trafficking, organized crime, and political terrorism. Whether nonmembership in WSIN/LEIU in fact hindered law enforcement in Seattle is an open question. To answer that question affirmatively is to argue that WSIN/LEIU and other information sharing networks provide useful information to the cooperating agencies. This point is very much in doubt. City Attorney Bernstein conceded that the ordinance did not even cover "most of the work of a metropolitan police force" (Bernstein, 1979: 94). Reviews by the Detroit Board of Police Commissioners (1979), the Michigan House of Representatives (1978), the U.S. General Accounting Office

(1979), and the U.S. Office of Technology Assistance (1982) all raised questions about the quality and utility of the information in the LEIU files and those of similar organizations.

The Seattle Police Department's view was supported by editorials in both Seattle daily newspapers (*Seattle Times*, April 8, 1982; *Seattle Post-Intelligencer*, May 3, 1982). Members of the coalition responded by arguing that there was no evidence that the Seattle Police Department had ever received any information of use in criminal investigations through LEIU. Furthermore, it noted that other law enforcement agencies had experienced audits of their LEIU files (Detroit, New York City, Chicago, Memphis) without being expelled from LEIU (Coalition on Government Spying, 1982).

In June 1982, the Seattle City Council amended the original ordinance to exempt files received by the Seattle Police Department from LEIU and WSIN from the auditor's review.[13] This exemption covered only those files related to organized criminal activity and narcotics trafficking. The auditor retained the authority to review all other files received from LEIU and WSIN. The chief of police assumed the responsibility for auditing the LEIU and WSIN files exempted from the auditor's review.

Whether this exemption represented a substantial weakening of the original ordinance is not clear. Although it created another potential loophole, the original ordinance contained ample loopholes if the police were determined to subvert the letter and spirit of the law. The significance of the 1982 modifications is perhaps more political than legal or administrative. After being on the defensive for eight years, the Seattle Police Department recovered support for their point of view from a majority of the city council and both of the daily newspapers.

The police department's stated objections to the operation of the ordinance pertained almost entirely to the problems of relations with other law enforcement agencies. The department has not argued that the ordinance has hindered its own investigatory work—that is, to develop information on its own about criminal activity in the city of Seattle. City Attorney Bernstein (1979: 94) adopted this view even before the ordinance took effect. He observed, "It was recognized during the legislative process that most of the daily work of a metropolitan police force would not be in the restricted information area, and, therefore, most of the paperwork and administrative burdens should be avoided."

The Auditor's Perspective

The Seattle police auditor reported full compliance with the ordinance during the law's first years. A personal interview with the auditor confirmed the impression given by his official reports: that compliance is high and the auditing process itself has settled into an uneventful bureaucratic routine. The first audit took several days, but more recent ones have taken only half a day. In sum, the present auditor feels that the ordinance is a reasonable device for controlling police conduct and that it has been effective in achieving its purposes. In particular, the law has a "sensitizing" effect on the police (Hoff, 1983; Seattle Police Auditor, 1981b).

The selection of an auditor presented a delicate political problem. The ordinance specified that the auditor be a person with, among other qualities, "a reputation for integrity and professionalism," "a commitment to and knowledge of the need for and responsibilities of law enforcement, as well as the need to protect basic constitutional rights" and "the potential for gaining the respect of departmental personnel and citizens of the City of Seattle." The person selected as the first auditor was a past president of the Washington State Bar Association and a practicing securities attorney with a large Seattle law firm. This individual represented a political compromise as he was deemed acceptable to both the coalition and the Seattle police. Hoff brought to his job no background experience with police matters. In a personal interview, he suggested that this was probably a virtue, given the fact that anyone with direct experience with police matters would, by virtue of that experience, have previously formed attitudes or personal contacts. Perhaps even more important, a person with previous experience as either prosecutor, criminal defense attorney, attorney for plaintiffs in police misconduct cases, or police union attorney would not be perceived as being neutral toward the police (Hoff, 1983).

The lack of experience with police matters does raise the question of whether the auditor could be misled by police officers. This point was raised with the current auditor. His view is that the police could indeed hide information from the auditor if they were determined to do so. He feels that the auditing process, however, has a general deterrent effect on misconduct. It sensitizes the police both to the importance of complying with the law and the principle of review by an outsider. The risk of disclosure by leak or some other process deters misconduct (Hoff, 1983).

The initial audit found a high level of compliance with the provisions of the ordinance. The auditor reported "(a) no substantial

violations of the ordinance, and (b) a good faith effort by the Seattle Police Department to comply with the ordinance in all respects" (Seattle Police Auditor, 1981b: 10). The police department made little use of the provisions of the ordinance. In the first year, only eleven authorizations for collecting restricted information were issued. Of the eleven, eight were "political authorizations" and three were "religious authorizations." None was extended beyond the original time frame and none resulted in criminal prosecutions. No authorizations for dignitary protection were issued nor were any infiltrators or informants authorized (Fitzsimons, 1981).

The auditor did note one ambiguity concerning the role of that office. On a few occasions, police officers solicited his advice about the propriety of particular actions. These requests placed the auditor in the de facto role of police legal advisor that meant giving prior approval to actions that he would subsequently have the responsibility of monitoring. The current auditor feels that this represents a serious role conflict and that the auditor should not be called upon for legal advice (Seattle Police Auditor, 1981a; Hoff, 1983).

CONCLUSIONS

After four years of operation, the Seattle Police Intelligence Ordinance appears to be a success, although certain questions and ambiguities remain.

On the positive side, the ordinance establishes two important principles: first, that police intelligence activities should be regulated by formal rules and that a legislative body can properly formulate those rules (Halperin, 1976); and, second, that police activities should be subject to regular review by an independent, external investigator. Unlike virtually every existing police review mechanism in the United States, which responds only to a complaint about police misconduct (Paulsen, 1970) the Seattle auditing process reviews routine police activities on a regular basis. It may be described as "proactive" rather than "reactive" and resembles the institutionalized inspection process in the U.S. military and the inspection of local police agencies by the British Home Office (Critchley, 1973). The ordinance does not appear to have hampered the legitimate criminal investigative activities of the Seattle police. Finally, the auditing process may well have a general deterrent effect on police misconduct.

Several questions remain, however. The first concerns the matter of willful violations by the police. Although the ordinance goes further than any existing mechanism in controlling police misconduct, the potential for willful evasion of the law and subversion of the

auditing process remains (Marx, 1982). Finally, the viability of the ordinance as a model for other agencies in the United States is problematic. Seattle participants appear unanimous in their belief that the local political environment was uniquely receptive to this pioneering ordinance. This environment includes a strong tradition of "open government" and the leadership role assumed by one key member of the city council. The political environments of the Congress, the fifty state legislatures, and the many city governments are not presently as supportive. The viability of the Seattle ordinance as a model for other law enforcement agencies depends largely on changes in these various political environments.[14]

NOTES

1. Seattle City Council, Ordinance #108333, July 2, 1979. For the sake of brevity, particular sections of the ordinance are not cited in this chapter.

2. The history of the spying scandal and the development of the ordinance is found in U.S. House of Representatives (1979).

3. (1) to other criminal justice agencies "in the performance of their official functions"; (2) persons "with a legitimate interest consent"; (3) persons with a lawful right to know under statute, regulation, or court order; (4) persons conducting academic or law enforcement research who give assurances of confidentiality; and, (5) regulatory agencies with a legitimate right to know.

4. (1) department personnel fields, (2) department internal investigations of its own personnel, (3) four categories of confidential communications as defined in the ordinance, (4) the personal files of the chief of police, and (5) specific case files that the King County prosecutor certifies in writing that must be withheld from the auditor because they involve investigations of government officials or might involve a conflict of interest on the part of the auditor, or investigations of organized crime.

5. This is to permit the individual to inspect his or her file and make a determination about suing for damages.

6. Even Seattle Police Chief Fitzsimons (1980) believes that the ordinance's supporters were more interested in the national impact of the law than the local.

7. See the relevant argument in James J. Fyfe (1982) with respect to the exclusionary rule.

8. Ordinance supporters prefer the term "chilling effect" to characterize the law's impact (Taylor, 1983).

9. City Attorney Bernstein (1979: 86) indicated that once the drafting process began, it was a foregone conclusion that an ordinance would be passed and his strategy was to "minimize the adverse effects" of such a law.

10. Stuart Scheingold's (1984) current research on the politics of law and order in Seattle may yield some answers to this question.

11. "It is the policy of the Seattle Police Department to cooperate fully with the Investigations Ordinance auditor." Seattle Police Department (n.d.b.:Section IX, A).

12. The anticipated passage of the ordinance led to another scandal. The lieutenant in charge of the Seattle Police Department intelligence unit transferred the LEIU intelligence cards in the department's possession to the Santa Clara Police Department

on the grounds that he "could no longer guarantee their security" (Schoener, 1978). The chief of the Santa Clara Police Department was then president of LEIU. This unauthorized action by the head of the intelligence unit came to light and aroused a small scandal. A departmental investigation officially exonerated the lieutenant in question, but he was transferred to the personnel unit, a move that represented an apparent slap on the wrist (*Seattle Post-Intelligencer*, July 1, 1978).

13. Ordinance #110640, June 17, 1982.

14. Some tentative evidence suggests that the advent of black political majorities in a number of major cities has changed local environments. With respect to Detroit, for example, see the concluding remark in Littlejohn (1981). Developments in Atlanta, Washington, D.C., and San Francisco (which involves the gay community as a major political force) merit investigation from this perspective.

REFERENCES

BERMAN, J. (1976) "A model statute for a charter for the F.B.I." Washington, DC: Center for National Security Studies.

BERNSTEIN, P. (1979) Testimony, U.S. House of Representatives, Subcommittee on Civil and Constitutional Rights, Judiciary Committee, 96th Cong. 1st and 2nd Sess. Hearings on H.R. 5030, Legislative Charter for the F.B.I.

Center for National Security Studies [CNSS] (1981) First Principles 6 (March/April): 1-2.

——— (1979) First Principles 5 (October): 1.

Center for Research on Criminal Justice (1977) The Iron Fist and the Velvet Glove. Berkeley, CA: Center for Research on Criminal Justice.

Coalition on Government Spying (1982) Memorandum, "Modifications to the police intelligence ordinance." (April 5)

——— (n.d.a) "LEIU/WSIN Memo."

——— (n.d.b) Principles for Effective Legislation. Seattle: Coalition on Government Spying.

CRITCHLEY, T. A. (1973) A History of Police in England and Wales. Montclair, NJ: Patterson Smith.

Detroit Board of Police Commissioners (1979) "An inquiry into the Detroit Police Department's membership in the Law Enforcement Intelligence Unit." (February 22).

FITZSIMONS, P. (1982) Personal communication.

——— (1981) Letter to Mayor Charles Royer (March 25).

——— (1980) "Interview." Law Enforcement News (April 7).

FYFE, J. (1982) "In search of the bad faith search." Criminal Law Bulletin 18 (May-June): 260-264.

GELLER, W. A. (1982) "Deadly force: What we know." Journal of Police Science and Administration 10, 2: 151-177.

HALPERIN, M. (1976) The Lawless State. New York: Penguin.

HOFF, D. (1983) Personal communication.

JURIS, H. and P. FEUILLE (1973) Police Unionism. Lexington, MA: Lexington.

LITTLEJOHN, E. (1981) "The civilian police commission: A deterrent to police misconduct." Journal of Urban Law, 59 (Fall): 5-62.

LOCKE, H. G. (1983) Personal communication.

MARX, G. (1982) "Who really gets stung?: Some issues raised by the new police undercover work." Crime and Delinquency (April): 165-193.

Michigan House of Representatives, Subcommittee on Privacy (1978) Memorandum, "The operation and organization structure of the law enforcement intelligence unit." (September 6).

PAULSEN, M. G. (1970) "Securing police compliance with constitutional limitations: The exclusionary rule and other devices," in Law and Order Reconsidered. New York: Bantam.

POTTS, L. (1983) Responsible Police Administration: Issues and Approaches. University, AL: University of Alabama Press.

REVELLE, R. (1979) Testimony in U.S. House of Representatives, Subcommittee on Civil and Constitutional Rights, Judiciary Committee, 96th Cong. 1st and 2nd Sess. Hearings on H.R. 5030, Legislative Charter for the FBI.

RUCHELMAN, L. (1974) Police Politics: A Comparative Study of Three Cities. Cambridge, MA: Ballinger.

RUXLOW, T. R. (1980) Letter to Patrick S. Fitzsimons, Chief of Police, Seattle Police Department. (October 29).

SCHEINGOLD, S. (1984) The Politics of Law and Order. New York: Longmans.

SCHOENER, R. G. (1978) Letter to Mr. Stan Carey, Santa Clara Police Department. (April 11).

Seattle Police Auditor (1981a) 18-Month Report to the Mayor and the Seattle City Council.

——— (1981b) Report of Police Intelligence Auditor (February 4).

Seattle Police Department (1979) "Training Bulletin 79-3" (August).

——— (n.d.a) Policy Manual.

——— (n.d.b) "Rules and Regulations for Investigations Ordinance."

TAYLOR, K. (1983) Personal communication.

——— (1979) Testimony, U.S. House of Representatives, Subcommittee on Civil and Constitutional Rights, Judiciary Committee, 96th Congress, 1st and 2nd Sessions. Hearings on H.R.5030, Legislative Charter for the FBI.

THOMAS, W. I. (1951) Social Behavior and Personality. New York: Social Science Research Council.

U.S. General Accounting Office (1980) The Multi-State Regional Intelligence Projects: Who Will Oversee These Federally Funded Networks? Report #GGD-81-36 (December 31).

——— (1979) The Interstate Organized Crime Index. Report #GGD-79-37 (May 25).

U.S. House of Representatives, Subcommittee on Civil and Constitutional Rights (1979) Judiciary Committee, 96th Cong., 1st and 2nd Sess. Hearings on H.R. 5030, Legislative Charter for the FBI. (September 12: 31-151).

U.S. Senate, Select Committee to Study Governmental Operations with Respect to Intelligence Activities (1976) 94th Cong. 1st and 2nd Sess. Hearings and Final Report.

U.S. Office of Technology Assessment (1982) An Assessment of Alternatives for a National Computerized Criminal History System (October).

WILSON, J. Q. (1973) The Varieties of Police Behavior. New York: Atheneum.

ABOUT THE AUTHORS

Timothy S. Bynum is currently a Visiting Professor at the Institute of Criminal Justice and Criminology at the University of Maryland and is also an Associate Professor in the School of Criminal Justice at Michigan State University. He received his Ph.D. in criminology from Florida State University in 1977 and has published a number of articles concerning decision making in the police court and correctional areas. He currently is conducting a study of intake and detention in juvenile courts and is involved in an evaluation of the impact of prison overcrowding legislation upon parole board decisions.

Francis T. Cullen received his Ph.D. (1979) in sociology and education from Columbia University and is currently Associate Professor of Criminal Justice and Sociology at the University of Cincinnati. His publications include *Rethinking Crime and Deviance Theory* (1983); *Reaffirming Rehabilitation* (1982); *Toward Paradigm of Labeling Theory* (1978); and the forthcoming *Corporate Crime Under Attack*. His research interests are in the areas of white-collar crime, criminal justice ideology, and prison reform.

David E. Duffee is currently a Visiting Professor of Social Systems Analysis at the State University of New York at Binghamton. He is on leave from the Graduate School of Criminal Justice, State University of New York at Albany, where he received his Ph.D. in 1973. He is interested in the relationship of community organizational structure and its effects on social control.

Erika S. Fairchild is an Associate Professor of Political Science and Public Administration at North Carolina State University, where she is also Director of the Master of Public Affairs Program. She teaches administration of justice and comparative systems of law and justice. Her recent research and publications have been in the field of criminal justice politics and comparative police administration.

Kim Montgomery Garrett received her B.A. in 1980 in sociology from Western Illinois University, where she is in the process of completing her master's degree. Currently, she is working for the Southern Coalition of Justice in Louisiana in an effort to prohibit capital punishment.

Jack R. Greene is an Associate Professor in the Department of Criminal Justice at Temple University. He received a Ph.D. in social science from Michigan State University in 1977, specializing in public policy and organizational analysis. His research has focused on police administration and operational decision making, the growth of criminal justice education and more recently the adequacy of evaluations of womens' performance in the police role. He is the editor of an anthology of papers on police management, *Managing Police Work* (Sage, 1982), and is currently involved in a study of police careers.

Dorothy Guyot is a Senior Research Associate at the Center for Policy Research in New York. Her research focus on police departments and hospitals inquires into improving the quality of service through improving management. She is the author of numerous articles on police management and has directed historical studies and survey research. A political scientist, Dr. Guyot received her Ph.D. from Yale in 1966 and her B.A. from the University of Chicago. She has taught at the Rutgers School of Criminal Justice, John Jay College of Criminal Justice of the City University of New York, Columbia University, and California Institute of Technology.

Anne M. Heinz, Assistant to the Dean of the Social Sciences Division, University of Chicago, received her B.A. from Wellesley and M.A. and Ph.D. in political science from Northwestern. She has taught at the University of Illinois at Chicago and Barat College and has held research appointments at the University of Chicago Law School and Northwestern. Her research has addressed a number of policy issues in the criminal justice area. She has published articles on innovations in plea bargaining and the legislative politics of criminal law. She is currently a member of the Board of Trustees of the Law and Society Association.

Albert P. Melone is an Associate Professor of Political Science at Southern Illinois University, Carbondale. He received his Ph.D. at the University of Iowa in 1972. He is the author of books, chapters in books, articles, reviews, and professional papers that focus upon interest group politics of legal professionals, judicial process and behavior, constitutional and administrative law, and interinstitutional conflict. His most recent co-authored book published in late 1984 by Palisades Publishers is entitled, *Bridges to Knowledge in Political Science: A Handbook for Research.*

Joel Rosch is an Assistant Professor of Political Science at North Carolina State University. He received his Ph.D. in political science at the University of Washington. He is currently working on a project comparing Japanese and American sentencing policy. His previous research has focused on sentencing policy in American courts.

Samuel Walker is Professor of Criminal Justice at the University of Nebraska at Omaha. He is the author of four books: *Sense and Nonsense About Crime* (1984); *The Police in America: An Introduction* (1983); *Popular Justice: A History of American Criminal Justice* (1980); and *A Critical History of Police Reform* (1977).

Vincent J. Webb is an Associate Professor of Criminal Justice at the University of Nebraska at Omaha. He is also Chairman of the Department of Criminal Justice and Director of the Center for Applied Urban Research. He has published in the areas of corrections, juvenile delinquency, sentencing, and criminal justice and criminology as developing academic fields.